Mohandas K. GANDHI
Thoughts, Words, Deeds
His Inspiration: BHAGAVAD-GITA

by

Ramnarine Sahadeo

Mohandas K. GANDHI
Thoughts Words Deeds
and His Inspiration: Bhagavad-Gita
by
Ramnarine Sahadeo

ISBN: 978-0-9868393-1-3

Printed at: reprographic and printing services
13/2, Rasoolpura, Secunderabad 500 003.
A P, INDIA

DEDICATION

To my life partner Jasmine; our children Bertrand and Tanya; and to my late mother Rosaline (1912–1999), married at age thirteen, widowed at age thirty-six when I was one year old, and to whom I am still trying to fulfill my promise by learning about her "way of life;" and to all practitioners of the universal ethic: TREAT OTHERS AS YOU WOULD LIKE TO BE TREATED.

AUTHORS PREFACE TO THE SECOND EDITION

The first edition of this book came out to mark the 10th anniversary of the atrocities of September 11, 2001 now popularly known as 9/11. It was primarily intended to show that we should not assume that thousands of years of human existence only produced one 9/11 and that we should not allow one dark event to dominate our thoughts, words or deeds each year. On the same date but in different years other men spoke of peace, love, and unity, in the face of some of the greatest injustices the world ever witnessed.

Hundreds of terrorist attacks killed thousands of people before and after this infamous day but they did not happen on AMERICAN SOIL and thus did not capture the attention of a world that has since restricted the freedoms and rights we once enjoyed. September 11 will find an indelible place in American History similar to the attack on Pearl Harbour. The latter however was initiated by a nation which later surrendered after a lengthy world war. It is much more difficult to confront and destroy an idea which motivated men to sacrifice their lives while killing others in the belief that the reward comes after death.

Those who once thought that Religion is a private matter between god and believer now have good reason to think again. When the towers in New York collapsed people of all religions lost their lives. Even agnostics and atheists were not spared. Consequently we must learn about all religions and how they can impact human behaviour and social development. While all religions may have some reference to TRUTH and PEACE there is no doubt that over the years, and particularly since the middle ages, there has been much destruction and loss of lives in HOLY WARS led by savages and tyrants who were supposed to have the blessings of GOD.

Whatever feeble attempts have been made to justify such acts it should be conceded that they were not caused because of poverty, exploitation, or lack of education, for there are millions across the globe who suffer from these daily.

Would a Supreme Being who created all mankind not be displeased with those who try to use scriptures which arose at different times of history, to show that some people and nations are favoured over others?

Are the favoured ones justified in using force to convert or to destroy the others who choose to refer to the Supreme Being by another name or worship him in a different way?

The answer would seem to be simple but not when we consider western history. Religion in its Western application divides people as it is conclusive and exclusionary leaving no space for those who do not share the same world view. This approach can be contrasted with the Eastern concept of DHARMA which makes room for all. Swami Vivekananda makes this quite clear in his speeches.

Mahatma Gandhi's views on Conversion are instructive since this widespread practice is still a hurdle in the attempt to find world peace. Whether done by the sword or by pen the notion of reaping souls has been described as an act of violence. There are fundamentalists and fanatics in all religions but they cannot be allowed to set the agenda for those who are willing to GIVE PEACE A CHANCE. Live and let live should be the guiding principle as it is more conducive to international harmony. The golden rule finds a central place in all religions and must be practiced not just recited. Each of us can refer to these when others on our own community try to germinate thoughts based on hate or fear, and which support violent and destructive behaviour.

The UNITED NATIONS UNIVERSAL DECLARATION OF HUMAN RIGHTS is an appendix so that it may be used as a guide to question any religious teachings which violate these fundamental principles. If religious leaders cannot give adequate answers to our questions, or invite us in private sessions to disrespect others, this it is time to look for another religion or join the greatest number of converts who are now AGNOSTICS or ATHEISTS, for they do less harm to humanity.

This edition also includes the complete speech of Mahatma Gandhi on September 11, 1906 in South Africa so the readers can appreciate his words in context and particularly the birth of the term SATYAGRAHA.

Swami Vivekananda's speeches at The Parliament of Religions commencing on September 11, 1893, are also added because readers wanted more that a summary of his bold attempt to bring Eastern philosophy to the West. It was his first trip to America and his efforts have sown the seeds of a value-system that is now bearing fruits and influencing lifestyles beyond Yoga, meditation, and vegetarianism. His lectures also support ancient universal principles for uniting those who can no longer find satisfactory answers in any religion that tells them not to respect the beliefs and peaceful practices of others.

The heart of this work is still Part 11 which Gandhi described as a BOOK OF UNIVERAL ETHICS, or principles of life; a summary of Vedic philosophy. It has been suggested that some may prefer to read Part 111 first as the many immortal comments and quotes in this section may serve as an inspiration and motivation encouraging the reader to delve into Part 11 again and again. No matter what our personality we will find an appropriate method to assist us in our spiritual growth as there are a variety of concepts in this literary treasure other than those in which Gandhi experimented and perfected.

The ultimate aim of this book can be summarised in Gandhi's own words. While he was fasting almost to death and was asked what do you want? His memorable reply was "I just want the fighting to stop". These were the exact words that a little child repeated to a family court judge who was presiding over the custody battle waged by her parents without regard to the harmful effects on her whom they both claim to love so much. Whether we are in a family conflict or one that will change the world we should reject any process that would destroy us in the end. The concept and practice of AHIMSA has far reaching effects and can be practiced in our own daily lives whether we occupy the most powerful offices in the world or whether we have the least important function in society. Surely It is the interest of all mankind to love, preserve, respect and protect all life forms on this planet and follow the footsteps of the great ones who knew that TO SERVE MAN IS TO SERVE GOD.

I wish to thank those who have expressed positive thoughts and insightful suggestions after reading the first edition, but particularly those whose level of awareness recognise that it is our global duty to oppose ignorance and violence by spreading this message of peace to all places of worship, every classroom, and eventually in every home.

Special appreciation to Leonard Dabydeen, friend, poet, civil rights activist, for his contribution to Part 111.

Ramnarine Sahadeo
Brampton, Ontario, Canada
2012
ramjihindu@rogers.com

TABLE OF CONTENTS

PART I

Namaste

This book is put together in appreciation of the one of the greatest souls of the twentieth century. If mankind is to change its current destructive direction, Gandhiji's message must remain a source of hope and inspiration if we are going to survive as a species.

Mohandas Karamchand Gandhi's (Mahatma) thoughts, words, and deeds empowered him with unimaginable influence that he used to make an indelible mark on world history. He was a spiritual leader with no political office but exercised more power than those in positions of authority because he was a visionary with an indomitable will and a potent force dedicated to social and political reform.

While countless books have been written about him and he penned his own autobiography *The Story Of My Experiments With Truth*, events since *September 11, 2001,* make this an appropriate time to relive his achievements in the hope that mankind can turn away from violence, anger, deceit, greed, and excessive materialism. These not only diminish us as rational human beings, but also hasten the destruction of all the progress that has been achieved over the centuries.

It should be self evident by now that ALL RELIGIONS ARE NOT THE SAME, although they do have similarities like the golden rule which forms an appendix at part 111.

Likewise all NINE ELVEVENs are not the same and hopefully the reader of this book would know that there are more NINE ELEVENs than 2001. And in future when the term is used it should be clear which NINE ELEVEN is being referred to: the one of hate, violence and division or the others that speak of love, nonviolence and universal brotherhood.

Gandhi's influence

We are all indebted to him, but few have expressed this more recently and eloquently than President Barack Obama in his 2010 address to a Joint Session of the Parliament of India:

I am mindful that I might not be standing here today, as President of the United States, had it not been for Gandhi and the message he shared with America and the rest of the world.

In response to the question who was the one person, living or dead, that he would chose to dine with, the president stated that it would be Gandhi, the person he admired a lot and who inspired Dr. King with his message of nonviolence. HE SAID THAT GANDHI CHANGED THE WORLD JUST BY THE POWER OF HIS ETHICS.

This was confirmed by Dr. King himself when he stated in 1955: "Christ gave us the goals, Gandhi gave us the tactics . . . Gandhi may have been the first person in history to lift the love ethic of Jesus above mere interaction between individuals to a powerful and effective social force on a large scale."

Leaders of political and social movements throughout the world had his writings and lifestyle to rely on in the struggles to improve the lot of their own people.

Former Polish President, Lech Walesa, former Zambian President Kenneth Kaunda, and Bangladeshi Nobel Laureate Mohammad Yunus are only some of the international leaders who agree that the message of peace of the "sacred warrior" will remain relevant and may be the key to human survival in the twenty-first century.

Anti-apartheid icon *Nelson Mandela* and South Africa's first black president in 1994 praised Gandhi's nonviolent approach, which contributed to the peaceful transformation and for healing the destructive human divisions that had been spawned by the abhorrent practice of apartheid. He reminded us that Gandhi's satyagraha began in Johannesburg where Gandhi practiced law and lived from 1893 to 1914. It has been stated that with respect to the ending of white rule in South Africa, Mandela finished what Gandhi started.

Other admirers included Steve Biko, Sung San Suu Kyi, Benigno Aquino Jr., Europe's Romain Rolland, Brazilian feminist Maria Lacerda de Moura, and of course Albert Einstein who accurately predicted that Gandhi will be a role model for generations to come. We have to be more concerned with his other prediction, which is that generations to come will hardly believe that one of flesh and blood actually walked on this earth. That time is already upon us, and therefore we must revisit his spirit and his teachings "my life is my message" and distribute throughout the globe the source of his inspiration.

Gandhi's Source of Inspiration

It is no secret that many were inspired by *The Mahatma*, but do we know what was his source of inspiration?

It is this little book of eighteen discourses (chapters) consisting of seven hundred slokas (verses) thousands of years old which teaches universal ethics and does not favor any sectarian point of view. Its lessons can still save us from inevitable self-immolation if we practice just a few principles therein. Regretfully, I have met too many, even from India, who still do not know that Gandhi's translation of this text exists.

While there are countless versions of the *Bhagvad Gita*, this version was preferred because *Mohandas Karamchand Gandhi* (Mahatma) lived it on a daily basis. It is recognized that this literary masterpiece is in some ways like a living constitution that lends itself to many interpretations as circumstances change over time. Comments and quotes are added to make reading a little more attractive for those who have not yet been exposed to this philosophical treasure. Material progress over the centuries has not been matched by man's spiritual growth. In this rapidly changing and violent world and particularly the events of the last hundred years, there ought to be no doubt that humanity still needs to rely on the wisdom of the Gita and the still unbelievable example of the simple, nonviolent lifestyle and character of a the saint with a bamboo staff.

The two words *Bhagvad* and *Gita* mean the song of the Lord. However, it is not a lyric but a philosophical poem and represents one of the earliest attempts of Indian thinkers to merge philosophy with religion. While it is one chapter of the great epic *Mahabharat*, and a summary of *Upanishadic teachings*, it can stand on its own. Its spiritual truths had a tremendous influence throughout history on religious and social reformers and many successful world leaders. In India itself, the Gita was a powerful weapon in the hands of progressive national leaders like *Tilak, Aurobindo Ghosh, and Gandhi* in their fight against British Imperialism. It suggests different ways to the supreme goal, is not rigid or sectarian, and its liberal outlook still makes it appealing to people of all faiths. In fact, the word *Hindu* never appears in the text, which Gandhi described as a book of universal ethics.

The setting is the battlefield of the ancient kingdom of Kurukshetra, about hundred miles from Delhi, where the Pandavas and their cousins, the Kauravas, more than five thousand years ago, faced each other on the eve of the *Mahabarat war*. The conflict resulted from a family dispute over the succession to the throne. Arjuna was overwhelmed with grief and refused to fight and kill his teachers, uncles, cousins, but his friend and charioteer, Krishna, a Hindu incarnation of God, in the philosophical and spiritual discourse that followed, persuaded him to do his duty as a Kshatriya warrior in a righteous war and detach himself from the results. To confuse this with a lecture on warfare however is a common error of those who have not read the entire text or know the circumstances leading up to the war. This immortal dialogue is rather an *instruction manual* telling us all how to live our lives on earth. It is particularly helpful in answering why we are here, what the goal of life is, and how to act when one's duty conflicts with another. In short, it shows the best way to attain self-realization (Moksha). Four paths (yoga) are recommended since humans differ in taste and temperament: *Karma* (action), *Raja* (meditation), *Bhakti* (devotion), and *Jnana Yoga* (knowledge). These interrelated paths all lead to the same goal.

There are hundreds of translations and interpretations of this eternal message, but this version should appeal to the vast majority of mankind as it is the contribution of the gentle but effective freedom fighter, the apostle of universal peace and brotherly love, *Mohandas Karamchand Gandhi.*

His concept of *Satyagraha* (resistance through mass civil disobedience based upon the foundation of nonviolence) which changed the course of world history can be found repeatedly in the Gita. These eternal teachings continue to inspire people of every race, religion, and nationality today. He described the seven sins affecting modern society as follows:

1. Politics without principles,
2. Wealth without work,
3. Pleasure without conscience,
4. Knowledge without character,
5. Commerce without morality,
6. Science without humanity,
7. Worship without sacrifice.

He practiced what he preached and used these principles in his first struggle to end the oppression in South Africa, put an end to the indentureship system wherever it existed in the British Empire, and finally in the greater struggle of Indian independence. He was one of the respected personalities of the twentieth century and no doubt will continue to influence the direction of mankind in this millennium. However, there are others who are already questioning whether this spiritual master with an indomitable will actually walked on this earth.

The First Years

Gandhiji was born on *October 2, 1869, in Porbandar, Gujarat, India,* and graced this world until an assassin's bullet ended his life on *January 30, 1948.*

In May 1883, when he was thirteen years old, he married fourteen-year-old Kasturbai Makhanji (Ba) in an arranged child marriage as was the custom.

In 1885, his father died and so did the couple's first child who lived for only a few days. They had four sons: Harilal born in 1888, Manilal born in 1892, Ramdass born 1897, and Devdas born in 1900.

On September 4, 1888, he left India to study law at University College, London. Before he left, he made a vow to his mother that he would observe the Hindu practice of abstaining from meat, alcohol, and promiscuity. There he met friends and studied both Hindu and Christian scriptures.

Unlike many who write and speak about *The Bhagavad-Gita*, Gandhi lived and experimented with those principles ever since two Englishmen induced him to read it during the second year of his studies in England. He was ashamed and felt miserable because even though he was born in India he knew nothing about Krishna's message of universal harmony and reverence for all forms of life.

On June 10, 1891, he was called to the Bar and left London for India only to learn that his mother had expired, but his family kept that bad news from him.

He tried unsuccessfully to establish a law practice in Bombay, then returned to Rajkot where he drafted petitions for litigants but was forced to stop by a British officer.

In 1893, he accepted a contract to work for an Indian firm in South Africa.

South Africa (1893–1914)

It is interesting to note that Gandhi qualified as a barrister by London's Inner Temple in 1891. After he was convicted on sedition charges in India, he was disbarred in 1922. The Bar of England and Wales restored his membership forty years after his death and sixty-six years after his disbarment.

One has to wonder how his life and the world would have been different if he was appointed a judge or just allowed to practice law and dress and live like any other British trained lawyer. But that was not to be.

The turning point in Gandhi's life was definitely his many experiences with discrimination in South Africa. It was not one single incident like the one when he was thrown off the train for refusing to move from first class to third class as immortalized by Hollywood. He was beaten by a driver for refusing to make room for a European traveler on a stagecoach. He was barred from several hotels. He refused to remove his turban in the courtroom when ordered to do so by a magistrate in Durban. After experiencing prejudice and witnessing social injustice firsthand, he began to question his role in life and his people's standing in the British Empire.

He helped to establish the Natal National Congress in 1894, an organization that was instrumental in unifying the community into a political force.

In 1897, he was attacked by a mob of white settlers, but the intervention of the wife of the superintendent of police saved him from harm, and then he refused to press charges consistent with the principle that he would not seek redress for a personal wrong in a court of law.

On September 11, 1906 (a 9/11 of peaceful protest), Gandhi adopted the first mass demonstration meeting involving the concept of satyagraha to oppose the passage of the law compelling registration of the colony's Indian population. The next seven years of struggle resulted in all forms of nonviolent protest, and eventually the public outcry over the harsh treatment of the peaceful protestors caused General Jan Christian Smuts to compromise with Gandhi. As the concept of satyagraha matured, its application became more and more refined and was the main weapon in the struggle for Indian Independence.

Religious Influence

Gandhi, like many great men, was a product of his experience, but his courage and convictions developed slowly.

He grew up in an India that was intensely religious and the ethical ideals of Islam, Christianity, and Jainism all influenced his outlook, but he never hesitated to call himself an orthodox Hindu. He wrote in *Young India* as early as October 6, 1921:

I call myself a *Sanatan* Hindu because:

1. I believe in the *Vedas, the Upanishads, the Puranas* and all that goes by the name of Hindu Scriptures, and therefore in *avatars* and rebirth;

2. I believe in the Varnashrama Dharma in a sense, in my opinion, strictly Vedic but not in its present popular and distorted crude sense;

3. I believe in the protection of the cow in its much larger sense than the popular; and

4. I do not disbelieve in murti puja.

The man who was to be called the Mahatma considered Hinduism to be a dynamic religion. The scriptural writings, he felt, grew out of the necessities of particular periods of history and seemed to conflict with others. They did not express new eternal truths but simply reflected how those principles were practiced at the time to which they belonged. He did not hesitate to oppose fanaticism and intolerance and to challenge the self-appointed defenders of Hinduism who attempted to justify religious bigotry, superstition, and outmoded practices. His battles for justice and equality for people of all social and economic backgrounds made him popular with the masses, gave hope to millions, and lit the fire for patriotism leading to revolts against injustice and oppression.

His unshakable faith in *God* as an indefinable power which transcended the senses and pervading all else was expressed as follows: "I do dimly perceive that whilst everything around me is changing, ever dying, there is underlying all this change a living power that is changeless, that holds all together, that creates, dissolves and recreates." He never thought of himself as perfect or as a *Mahatma,* and he probably anticipated many critics by relating his own failures and shortcomings in his autobiography.

Man, he stated, is capable of being good and compassionate, and when he commits evil he goes astray or is misled by false teachings or corrupt leaders, but it is for man to look within himself to find that spark of divinity. The way to find God was to see him in all creation.

Gandhi himself felt that the road to salvation lay through *his love for humanity* and everything that lived. Killing of animals is not necessary for man's survival, and many who are vegetarians today are keenly aware of this fact.

His concern about not abusing resources was not limited to material things but even led him to reduce his use of words.

He did not speak for one day per week, and if he had to communicate, he resorted to writing.

Mediation and quiet even for a few hours should be a universal practice consistent with the thought that *one should not open one's mouth unless the spoken words would improve on the silence.*

While there are many verses in the Gita that will appeal to different personalities, Chapter 17, verses 14–16, was chosen as a title to this book since they relate to austerities of thought, word, deed, all practiced by the great soul. These refer to purity, honesty, celibacy, and nonviolence (deed); non-offensive, truthful, pleasant, and beneficial speech (word); and serenity of mind, gentleness, equanimity, self-restraint, silence, and purity of the mind (thought).

In *Young India* of March 3, 1925, he defines *God* as "truth and love, ethics and morality, fearlessness, the source of all light and life, yet higher than and beyond all these." He also described *truth as God.*

Truth was subjective, abstract, and irrational: "What a pure heart feels at a particular time is *Truth*; by remaining firm on that, undiluted Truth can be attained."

This allowed him to define truth as love and then love as *nonviolence (ahimsa)*, which is the highest form of ethics. Ahimsa comes before Swaraj (self-rule) and must be placed before everything else, then it becomes *irresistible.*

Some mistake Gandhi's nonviolence as a negative principle, encouraging cowardice and passivity.

On the contrary, he insists that only the active and courageous could really become nonviolent, a concept that cannot be taught to the person who fears to die and has no power of resistance. It does not mean meek submission to evil or the evildoer. Rather, it means putting one's whole soul against the will of the tyrant. Thus, it was possible for one person to defy the tyranny of a mighty, unjust empire. The principle of nonviolence was his most potent weapon in the struggle against imperialism as thousands of men and women bravely faced arrest, assault, bullets, and even death in the mass resistance to British rule.

It is a principle that was practiced by many other leaders and freedom movements across the globe since it was perfected by Gandhi because nonviolence is one of those universal eternal principles of *Sanatan Dharma* that could be applied anywhere. There is no doubt that we will continue to witness this approach as people of all nations struggle for freedom and self-determination, recognizing that they will have greater support than those who resort to violence, which may only result in temporary victory. The end and the means must be the same for there to be a permanent change, and both must be grounded in morality according to the Mahatma.

The technique of nonviolence was *satyagraha* (truth force). The satyagrahi recognizes that the tyrant has power over his body and material possessions, but not his soul. As the Gita states, the body can be imprisoned or destroyed, but the soul remains unconquered and unconquerable. The whole science of satyagraha was born from knowledge of this fundamental truth. However, it takes courage and involves suffering. The satyagrahi must possess certain essential virtues, namely, truth, nonviolence, abstinence, non-stealing, non-possessiveness, simple living, and faith in God. Class struggles did not appeal to Gandhi, who believed that the moral ideals he prescribed applied to all peoples and to all conditions of society, and that society could be changed through the moral and spiritual strength of individuals without altering the relations of production and the system of class exploitation. Religion, he thought, was a force which could safeguard the interest of the masses, but it had to be connected to daily life or was useless. The theory of satyagraha was his attempt to introduce religion into the realm of politics. There can be no doubt that while these ethical principles were intended for the moral and spiritual purification of the individual, it had a greater impact on the social awakening of India.

On Communism

Gandhi worked for economic equality but believed that capital and labor can cooperate to avoid the violence and force that he opposed observed in the Communist system. "The classless society is worth striving for but not if force is used to achieve this end . . . we are all born equal but for centuries resisted the will of god. The idea of inequality of 'high and low' is an evil, but I do not believe in eradicating evil from the human breast at the point of a bayonet," he stated. Consequently, he espoused the *trusteeship doctrine* whereby capitalists and landlords had the divine responsibility of looking after the interests of workers and peasants. While this doctrine was severely criticized, it must be conceded that religio-ethical theories awakened a new consciousness in the masses since socio-economic conditions were such that the workers had not yet attained significant class consciousness.

On Conversion

He lived a life dictated by the Gita and called himself an orthodox Hindu; he respected all other religions, but vehemently opposed religious conversion. One of his earthly possessions included a book *The Life and Teachings of Jesus*. Many who claim to be Christians must have forgotten this, for Gandhi made a clear distinction between practice and preaching when he said, "I like your Christ, I do not like your Christians. Your Christians are so unlike your Christ." He found it inconceivable that Christ would have approved modern Christian organizations, public worship, or ministry. He concluded that all religions were true and that all had some errors in them, but the goal should be to convert others but to pray that a Hindu should become a better Hindu, a Muslim a better Muslim, a Christian a better Christian (*Young India*, January 19, 1928).

However, all religions have something in common, and Gandhi's monument in New Belgrade, Serbia, says it in a nutshell that "the essence of all religions is nonviolence."

God, he stated, had no religion, and he could safely state that he was a Hindu, a Christian, a Muslim, a Buddhist, and a Jew. In South Africa, he called on the Indians to follow "Gentle Jesus the greatest passive resister the world has even seen." He often referred to his love for the *Sermon on the Mount* (see Appendix), and he believed in Hindu–Muslim unity and died for that cause. After he was shot by a fanatic Hindu on January 30, 1948, consistent with his belief that God should always be in our minds (Gita, Chapter 8: 5–6), he reportedly uttered his final words *He Ram* (O god)!

His numerous comments on conversion form an appendix to this book as they too are still germane today and apply to any form by any religious group although his comments were based on the India of his time when it was linked to imperialism.

Gita Reaches the West

Enlightened humanists such as *Ralph Waldo Emerson* and *Henry David Thoreau* may have been the first to refer to this literary masterpiece in the Western world. However, it was not until *May 5, 1838,* that significant numbers of Gita practitioners took this value system to South America when two ships, the *Whitby and the Hesperus,* transported indentured servants from India to British Guiana (Guyana). Indians were already in Mauritius by 1834.

These children of Bharat were later transplanted to many other lands and learnt English, French, Dutch, and Spanish in order to survive. Those countries include Trinidad, Guadeloupe, Jamaica, Surinam, Grenada, St. Kitts, St. Lucia, Martinique, St. Vincent, French Guiana, St. Croix, and Cuba. There is evidence suggesting that after the great *Indian Mutiny of 1857,* sepoys and their families were deported to British Honduras (Belize). Today they can be found all over South America.

In the early nineteenth century, it was stated that the *sun never sets on the British Empire* for it had colonies from the Caribbean to South Pacific, where Indian indentured laborers were sent to replace slaves on the plantations. Thus, Vedic values also traveled to countries like Fiji, Sri Lanka, Burma, South Africa, and Mauritius.

This process continued until 1917 when the last immigrant ship S.S. Ganges arrived in Guyana. Mahatma Gandhi and others from the Indian National Congress successfully opposed this practice called slavery under a different name. However, by that time over one million Indians had been dispersed all over the globe and approximately half a million came to Guyana and the Caribbean. Today a few of these countries have villages which remind one of *"Little India"* while others have surrendered to environmental forces over the years and has little connection with *Bharat Mata.*

Nine Elevens Distinguished

The birth of peaceful protest SATYAGRAGHA on September 11, 1906 has not sustained its rightful prominence in history but we now have ample reason to inform and remind ourselves of it significance.

Many of us sat in our living rooms and watched in disbelief as the events of *September 11, 2001,* unfolded before our eyes as the twin towers in New York collapsed, taking with them thousands of lives. Many of us were left with horror and the belief that mankind will forever be involved in internecine conflict. However, if we are to remain hopeful and positive, the date that should be indelibly etched in our minds should be the events of an earlier 9/11. We cannot surrender to hate and violence when we have so many positive events and personalities who should be equally etched in our psyche.

On *September 11, 1893,* North America was first introduced to the unifying potential of the Gita's universal message. It was on that day that the dynamic *Swami Vivekananda* addressed The Parliament of Religions in Chicago and planted the seeds of a philosophy of love and peace desired by the vast majority of mankind:

> *The present convention, which is one of the most august assemblies ever held, is itself a vindication, a declaration to the world, of the wonderful doctrine preached in the Gita:*
>
> *Whosoever comes to Me, through whatsoever form,*
> *I reach him;*
>
> *All men struggling through paths which in the end lead to Me.*

Sectarianism, bigotry, and its horrible descendant, fanaticism, have long possessed this beautiful earth. They have filled the earth with violence, drenched it often and often with human blood, destroyed civilization, and sent whole nations to despair. Had it not been for these horrible demons, human society would be far more advanced than it is now. But their time is come; and I fervently hope that the bell that tolled this morning in honor of this convention may be the death-knell of all fanaticism, of all persecutions with the sword or with the pen, and of all uncharitable feelings between persons wending their way to the same goal.

Regretfully we have not seen the death-knell envisioned by this spiritual icon, but this does not mean that the philosophy he espoused has lost its relevance. Mankind still has to learn and practice its precepts. The universal teachings are now all over the globe and remain a potent force in cultures and places where Gandhi never visited.

Today the landscape of most major cities in Canada, USA, and Europe are dotted with numerous awe-inspiring temples which will hopefully help to spread the message of love and peace. However, there is great concern that material plenty, ignorance, short-sightedness, and the thirst for immediate gratification will cause many to depart from the wisdom and spiritual values that are the very foundation of the Vedic Saraswati civilization.

Hopefully, the Gita will continue to guide posterity as it served their ancestors, thereby fulfilling the dreams of men like Chakravarti Rajagopalachari, associate and conscience keeper of the Mahatma. He opined that a liberal education means an attainment of a sound knowledge of the great religious philosophy for which India is famous throughout the civilized world. The Bhagavad-Gita is the core of that knowledge.

It is interesting to note that the method of teaching known as the Socratic method may more accurately be called *The Krishna Method* with its origins in the Gita. The pattern was laid down by Lord Krishna as he taught Arjuna one answer at a time as the lessons become more interesting, but in the end left the latter to make his own decisions. This we all must do in fighting our internal battles on a daily basis.

It is hoped that the reader will still find this ancient text an ethical guide while demonstrating to mankind how one can struggle incessantly against injustice without resorting to violence that results in death to innocent victims or destruction of property. One does not even have to get angry in order to perform this duty once the level of consciousness is attained.

Gandhi displayed every form of courage to the highest possible degree. He suffered all kinds of punishments, disappointments, and tragedies, but those have not left any permanent scars, a fact that he credits to the Gita.

One memorable characteristic of Gandhi was his infectious laugh and his great wit. As he was going to meet King George V at Buckingham palace, he was asked whether his white sheet and loincloth were enough clothing for a royal reception, and he answered, "The king has enough on for both of us."

Even when sentenced to six years, he thanked the judge for his fairness and courtesy, joyfully going to prison where he became close friends with his jailors and was happy as a bird spending most of his time in quiet contemplation and writing.

He was certainly among the greatest conservationists that we know about. He wore very little, spoke few words and kept silent for long periods when necessary, ate small portions, lived on vegetables and goat's milk, and recycled when possible.

If we live and let others live and have mutual respect for each other irrespective of race, religion, nationality, social group, or political views, we may still see the Ram Raj that this soldier of peace dreamt of.

We can remind posterity of his existence and achievements by having his birthday October 2 celebrated as an International day of Peace and Love. We can also establish many institutions of higher learning in his name.

Those of us who lived during his lifetime or admire his achievements owe this duty to future generations.

Namaste

Ramnarine Sahadeo

www.dharmaeducation.info

ramjihindu@rogers.com

PART 2

The Bhagavad-Gita

Introduction

It was at Kosani in Almora on June 24, 1929, i.e., after two years' waiting, that I finished the introduction to my translation of the Gita. The whole was then published in due course. It has been translated in Hindi, Bengali, and Marathi. There has been an insistent demand for an English translation. I finished the translation of the introduction at the Yeravda prison. Since my discharge it has lain with friends and now I give it to the reader. Those, who take no interest in the Book of Life, will forgive the trespass on these columns. To those who are interested in the poem and treat it as their guide in life, my humble attempt might prove of some help. —MKG)

1. Just as, acted upon by the affection of coworkers like Swami Anand and others, I wrote *My Experiments with Truth*, so has it been regarding my rendering of the Gita. "We shall be able to appreciate your meaning of the message of the Gita, only when we are able to study a translation of the whole text by yourself, with the addition of such notes as you may deem necessary. I do not think it is just on your part to deduce ahimsa etc. from stray verses," thus spoke Swami Anand to me during the noncooperation days. I felt the force of his remarks. I, therefore, told him that I would adopt his suggestion when I got the time. Shortly afterwards I was imprisoned. During my incarceration I was able to study the Gita more fully. I went reverently through the Gujarati translation of Lokamanya's great work. He had kindly presented me with the Marathi original and the translations in Gujarati and Hindi, and had asked me, if I could not tackle the original, at least to go through the Gujarati translation. I had not been able to follow the advice outside the prison walls. But when I was imprisoned I read the Gujarati translation. This reading whetted my appetite for more and I glanced through several works on the Gita.

2. My first acquaintance with the Gita began in 1888–89 with the verse translation by Sir Edwin Arnold known as *The Song Celestial*.

On reading it, I felt a keen desire to read a Gujarati translation. And I read as many translations as I could lay hold of. But all such reading can give me no passport for presenting my own translation. Then again my knowledge of Sanskrit is limited, my knowledge of Gujarati too is in no way scholarly. How could I then dare present the public with my translation?

3. It has been my endeavor, as also that of some companions, to reduce to practice the teaching of the Gita as I have understood it. The Gita has become for us a spiritual reference book. I am aware that we ever fail to act in perfect accord with the teaching. The failure is not due to want of effort, but is in spite of it. Even though the failures we seem to see rays of hope. The accompanying rendering contains the meaning of the Gita message which this little band is trying to enforce in its daily conduct.

4. Again this rendering is designed for women, the commercial class, the so-called Shudras and the like who have little or no literary equipment, who have neither the time nor the desire to read the Gita in the original and yet who stand in need of its support. In spite of my Gujarati being unscholarly, I must own to having the desire to leave to the Gujaratis, through the mother tongue, whatever knowledge I may possess. I do indeed wish that at a time when literary output of a questionable character is pouring upon the Gujaratis, they should have before them a rendering the majority can understand of a book that is regarded as unrivalled for its spiritual merit and so withstand the overwhelming flood of unclean literature.

5. This desire does not mean any disrespect to the other renderings. They have their own place. But I am not aware of the claim made by the translators of enforcing their meaning of the Gita in their own lives. At the back of my reading there is the claim of an endeavor to enforce the meaning in my own conduct for an unbroken period of forty years. For this reason I do indeed harbor the wish that all Gujarati men or women wishing to shape their conduct according to their faith, should digest and derive strength from the translation here presented.

6. My coworkers, too, have worked at this translation. My knowledge of Sanskrit being very limited, I should not have full confidence in my literal translation. To that extent, therefore, the translation has passed before the eyes of Vinoba, Kaka Kalelkar, Mahadev Desai and Kishorlal Mashruwala.

7. Now about the message of the Gita.

8. Even in 1888–89, when I first became acquainted with the Gita, I felt that it was not a historical work, but that, under the guise of physical warfare, it described the duel that perpetually went on in the hearts mankind, and that physical warfare was brought in merely to make the description of the internal duel more alluring. This preliminary intuition became more confirmed on a closer study of religion and the Gita. A study of the Mahabharata gave it added confirmation. I do not regard the Mahabharata as a historical work in the accepted sense. The Adiparva contains powerful evidence in support of my opinion. By ascribing to the chief actors superhuman or subhuman origins, the great Vyasa made short work of the history of kings and their peoples. The persons therein described may be historical, but the author of the Mahabharata has used them merely to drive home his religious theme.

9. The author of the Mahabharata has not established the necessity of physical warfare; on the contrary he has proved its futility. He has made the victors shed tears of sorrow and repentance, and has left them nothing but a legacy of miseries.

10. In this great work the Gita is the crown. Its second chapter, instead of teaching the rules of physical warfare, tells us how a perfected man is to be known. In the characteristics of the perfected man of the Gita, I do not see any to correspond to physical warfare. Its whole design is inconsistent with the rules of conduct governing the relations between warring parties.

11. Krishna of the Gita is perfection and right knowledge personified; but the picture is imaginary. That does not mean that Krishna, the adored of his people, never lived. But perfection is imagined. The idea of a perfect incarnation is an after growth.

12. In Hinduism, incarnation is ascribed to one who has performed some extraordinary service of mankind. All embodied life is in reality an incarnation of God, but it is not usual to consider every living being an incarnation. Future generations pay this homage to one who, in his own generation, has been extraordinarily religious in his conduct. I can see nothing wrong in this procedure; it takes nothing from God's greatness, and there is no violence done to Truth. There is an Urdu saying which means, "Adam is not God but he is a spark of the Divine." And therefore he who is the most religiously behaved has most of the divine spark in him. It is in accordance with this train of thought that Krishna enjoys, in Hinduism, the status of the most perfect incarnation.

13. This belief in incarnation is a testimony of man's lofty spiritual ambition. Man is not at peace with himself till he has become like unto God. The endeavor to reach this state is the supreme, the only ambition worth having. And this is self-realization. This self-realization is the subject of the Gita, as it is of all scriptures. But its author surely did not write it to establish that doctrine. The object of the Gita appears to me to be that of showing the most excellent way to attain self-realization. That which is to be found, more or less clearly, spread out here and there in Hindu religious books, has been brought out in the clearest possible language in the Gita even at the risk of repetition.

14. That matchless remedy is renunciation of fruits of action.

15. This is the centre round which the Gita is woven. This renunciation is the central sun, round which devotion, knowledge, and the rest revolve like planets. The body has been likened to a prison. There must be action where there is body. Not one embodied being is exempted from labor. And yet all religions proclaim that it is possible for man, by treating the body as the temple of God, to attain freedom. Every action is tainted, be it ever so trivial. How can the body be made the temple of God? In other words how can one be free from action, i.e., from the taint of sin? The Gita has answered the question in decisive language: "By desireless action; by renouncing fruits of action; by dedicating all activities to God, i.e., by surrendering oneself to Him body and soul."

16. But desirelessness or renunciation does not come for the mere talking about it. It is not attained by intellectual feat. It is attainable only by a constant heart-churn. Right knowledge is necessary for attaining renunciation. Learned men possess a knowledge of a kind. They may recite the Vedas from memory, yet they may be steeped in self-indulgence. In order that knowledge may not run riot, the author of the Gita has insisted on devotion accompanying it and has given it the first place. Knowledge without devotion will be like a misfire. Therefore, says the Gita, "Have devotion, and knowledge will follow." This devotion is not mere lip worship, it is a wrestling with death. Hence, the Gita's assessment of the devotee's quality is similar to that of the sage.

17. Thus the devotion required by the Gita is no soft-hearted effusiveness. It certainly is not blind faith. The devotion of the Gita has the least to do with the externals. A devotee may use, if he likes, rosaries, forehead marks, make offerings, but these things are no test of his devotion. He is the devotee who is jealous of none, who is a fount of mercy, who is without egotism, who is selfless, who treats alike cold and heat, happiness, and misery, who is ever forgiving, who is always contented, whose resolutions are firm, who has dedicated mind and soul to God, who causes no dread, who is not afraid of others, who is free from exultation, sorrow and fear, who is pure, who is versed in action and yet remains unaffected by it, who renounces all fruit, good or bad, who treats friend and foe alike, who is untouched by respect or disrespect, who is not puffed up by praise, who does not go under when people speak ill of him who loves silence and solitude, who has a disciplined reason. Such devotion is inconsistent with the existence at the same time of strong attachments.

18. We thus see that to be a real devotee is to realize oneself. Self-realization is not something apart. One rupee can purchase for us poison or nectar, but knowledge or devotion cannot buy us salvation or bondage. These are not media of exchange. They are themselves the thing we want. In other words, if the means and the end are not identical, they are almost so. The extreme of means is salvation. Salvation of the Gita is perfect peace.

19. But such knowledge and devotion, to be true, have to stand the test of renunciation of fruits of action. Mere knowledge of right and wrong will not make one fit for salvation. According to common notions, a mere learned man will pass as a pandit. He need not perform any service. He will regard as bondage even to lift a little lota. Where one test of knowledge is nonliability for service, there is no room for such mundane work as the lifting of a lota.

20. Or take bhakti. The popular notion of bhakti is soft-heartedness, telling beads and the like, and disdaining to do even a loving service, least the telling of beads etc. might be interrupted. This bhakti, therefore, leaves the rosary only for eating, drinking and the like, never for grinding corn or nursing patients.

21. But the Gita says: No one has attained his goal without action. Even men like Janaka attained salvation through action. If even I were lazily to cease working, the world would not perish. How much more necessary then for the people at large to engage in action.

22. While on the one hand it is beyond dispute that all action binds, on the other hand it is equally true that all living beings have to do some work, whether they will or no. Here all activity, whether mental or physical is to be included in the term action. Then how is one to be free from the bondage of action, even though he may be acting? The manner in which the Gita has solved the problem is to my knowledge unique. The Gita says: "Do your allotted work but renounce its fruit—be detached and work—have no desire for reward and work." This is the unmistakable teaching of the Gita. He who gives up action falls. He who gives up only the reward rises. But renunciation of fruit in no way means indifference to the result. In regard to every action one must know the result that is expected to follow, the means thereto, and the capacity for it. He, who, being thus equipped, is without desire for the result and is yet wholly engrossed in the due fulfillment of the task before him is said to have renounced the fruits of his action.

23. Again let no one consider renunciation to mean want of fruit for the renouncer. The Gita reading does not warrant such a meaning.

Renunciation means absence of hankering after fruit. As a matter of fact, he who renounces reaps a thousandfold. The renunciation of the Gita is the acid test of faith. He who is ever brooding over result often loses nerve in the performance of his duty. He becomes impatient and then gives vent to anger and begins to do unworthy things; he jumps from action to action never remaining faithful to any. He who broods over results is like a man given to objects of senses; he is ever distracted, he says good-bye to all scruples, everything is right in his estimation and he therefore resorts to means fair and foul to attain his end.

24. From the bitter experiences of desire for fruit the author of the Gita discovered the path of renunciation of fruit and put it before the world in a most convincing manner. The common belief is that religion is always opposed to material good. "One cannot act religiously in mercantile and such other matters. There is no place for religion in such pursuits; religion is only for attainment of salvation," we hear many worldly-wise people say. In my opinion the author of the Gita has dispelled this delusion. He has drawn no line of demarcation between salvation and worldly pursuits. On the contrary he has shown that religion must rule even our worldly pursuits. I have felt that the Gita teaches us that what cannot be followed out in day-to-day practice cannot be called religion. Thus, according to the Gita, all acts that are incapable of being performed without attachment are taboo. This golden rule saves mankind from many a pitfall. According to this interpretation murder, lying, dissoluteness and the like must be regarded as sinful and therefore taboo. Man's life then becomes simple, and from that simpleness springs peace.

25. Thinking along these lines, I have felt that in trying to enforce in one's life the central teaching of the Gita, one is bound to follow Truth and ahimsa. When there is no desire for fruit, there is no temptation for untruth or himsa. Take any instance of untruth or violence, and it will be found that at its back was the desire to attain the cherished end. But it may be freely admitted that the Gita was not written to establish ahimsa. It was an accepted and primary duty even before the Gita age. The Gita had to deliver the message of renunciation of fruit. This is clearly brought out as early as the second chapter.

26. But if the Gita believed in ahimsa or it was included in desirelessness, why did the author take a warlike illustration? When the Gita was written, although people believed in ahimsa, wars were not only not taboo, but nobody observed the contradiction between them and ahimsa.

27. In assessing the implications of renunciation of fruit, we are not required to probe the mind of the author of the Gita as to his limitations of ahimsa and the like. Because a poet puts a particular truth before the world, it does not necessarily follow that he has known or worked out all its great consequences or that having done so, he is able always to express them fully. In this perhaps lies the greatness of the poem and the poet. A poet's meaning is limitless. Like man, the meaning of great writings suffers evolution. On examining the history of languages, we noticed that the meaning of important words has changed or expanded.

This is true of the Gita. The author has himself extended the meanings of some of the current words. We are able to discover this even on superficial examination. It is possible that, in the age prior to that of the Gita, offering of animals as sacrifice was permissible. But there is not a trace of it in the sacrifice in the Gita sense. In the Gita continuous concentration on God is the king of sacrifices. The third chapter seems to show that sacrifice chiefly means body-labor for service. The third and fourth chapters read together will use other meanings for sacrifice, but never animal sacrifice. Similarly has the meaning of the word sannyasa undergone, in the Gita, a transformation. The sannyasa of the Gita will not tolerate complete cessation of all activity.

The sannyasa of the Gita is all work and yet no work. Thus the author of the Gita, by extending meanings of words, has taught us to imitate him. Let it be granted, that according to the letter of the Gita it is possible to say that warfare is consistent with renunciation of fruit. But after forty years' unremitting endeavor fully to enforce the teaching of the Gita in my own life, I have in all humility felt that perfect renunciation is impossible without perfect observance of ahimsa in every shape and form.

28. The Gita is not an aphoristic work; it is a great religious poem. The deeper you dive into it, the richer the meanings you get. It being meant for the people at large, there is pleasing repetition. With every age the important words will carry new and expanding meanings. But its central teaching will never vary. The teacher is at liberty to extract from this treasure any meaning he likes so as to enable him to enforce in his life the central teaching.

29. Nor is the Gita a collection of do's and don'ts. What is lawful for one may be unlawful for another. What may be permissible at one time, or in one place, may not be so at another time, and in another place. Desire for fruit is the only universal prohibition. Desirelessness is obligatory.

30. The Gita has sung the praises of Knowledge, but it is beyond the mere intellect; it is essentially addressed to the heart and capable of being understood by the heart. Therefore the Gita is not for those who have no faith. The author makes Krishna say: "Do not entrust this treasure to him who is without sacrifice, without devotion, without the desire for this teaching and who denies Me. On the other hand, those who will give this precious treasure to My devotees will, by the fact of this service, assuredly reach me. And those who, being free from malice, will with faith absorb this teaching, shall, having attained freedom, live where people of true merit go after death."

Mohandas Karamchand Gandhi at 7 (1876).

Discourse 1: Arjuna's Gloom and Question

Dhritarashtra Said:

1. Tell me, O Sanjaya, what my sons and Pandu's assembled, on battle intent, did on the field of Kuru, the field of duty.

   The human body is the battlefield where the eternal duel between right and wrong goes on. Therefore it is capable of being turned into a gateway to Freedom. It is born in sin and becomes the seed-bed of sin. Hence it is also called the field of Kuru. The Kuravas represent the forces of Evil, the Pandavas the forces of Good. Who is there that has not experienced the daily conflict within himself between the forces of Evil and the forces of Good?

Sanjaya Said:

2. On seeing the Pandava's army drawn up in battle array, King Duryodhana approached Drona, the preceptor, and addressed him thus:

3. Behold, O preceptor, this mighty army of the sons of Pandu, set in array by the son of Drupada, thy wise disciple.

---

* The best way to find yourself is to lose yourself in the service of others.

4. Here are brave bowmen, peers of Bhima and Arjuna in fighting: Yuyudhana and Virata, and the "Maharatha" Drupada.

5. Dhrishtaketu, Chekitana, valorous Kashiraja, Purujit the Kuntibhoja, and Shaibya, chief among men.

6. Valiant Yudhamanyu, valorous Uttamaujas, Subhadra's son, and the sons of Draupadi—each one of them a "Maharatha."

7. Acquaint thyself now, O best of Brahmanas, with the distinguished among us. I mention for thy information, the names of the captains of my army.

8. Thy noble self, Bhishma, Karna, and Kripa, victorious in battle, Ashvatthaman, Vikarna, also Somadatta's son;

9. There is many another hero, known for his skill in wielding diverse weapons, pledged to lay down his life for my sake, and all adepts in war.

10. This our force, commanded by Bhishma, is all too inadequate; while theirs, commanded by Bhima, is quite adequate.

11. Therefore, let each of you, holding your appointed places, at every entrance, guard only Bhishma.

12. At this, the heroic grandsire, the grand old man of the Kurus, gave a loud lion's roar and blew his conch to hearten Duryodhana.

13. Thereupon, conches, drums, cymbals, and trumpets were sounded all at once. Terrific was the noise.

14. Then Madhava and Pandava, standing in their great chariot yoked with white steeds, blew their divine conches.

15. Hrishikesha blew the Panchajanya and Dhananjaya the Devadatta; while the wolfbellied Bhima of dread deeds sounded his great conch Paundra.

16. King Yudhishthira, Kunti's son, blew the Anantavijaya, and

Nakula and Sahadeva their conches, Sughosha and Manipushpaka.

17. And Kashiraja, the great bowman, Shikhandi the "Maharatha," Dhrishtadyumna, Virata, and Satyaki, the unconquerable;

18. Drupada, Draupadi's sons, the strong-armed son of Subhadra, all these, O King, blew each his own conch.

19. That terrifying tumult, causing earth and heaven to resound, rent the hearts of Dhritarashtra's sons.

20–21. Then, O King, the ape-bannered Pandava, seeing Dhritarashtra's sons arrayed and flight of arrows about to begin, took up his bow, and spoke thus to Hrishikesha: "Set my chariot between the two armies, O Achyuta!"

22. That I may behold them drawn up, on battle intent, and know whom I have to engage in this fearful combat;

23. And that I may survey the fighters assembled here anxious to fulfill in battle perverse Duryodhana's desire.

Sanjaya said:

24–25. Thus addressed by Gudakesha, O King, Hrishikesha set the unique chariot between the two armies in front of Bhishma, Drona and all the kings and said: Behold, O Partha, the Kurus assembled yonder.

26–28. Then did Partha see, standing there, sires, grandsires, preceptors, uncles, brothers, sons, grandsons, comrades, fathers-in-law and friends in both armies. Beholding all these kinsmen ranged before him, Kaunteya was overcome with great compassion and spake thus in anguish:

Arjuna said:

28–29. As I look upon these kinsmen, O Krishna, assembled here eager to fight, my limbs fail, my mouth is parched, a tremor shakes my frame and my hair stands on end.

30. Gandiva slips from my hand, my skin is on fire, I cannot keep my feet, and my mind reels.

31. I have unhappy forebodings, O Keshava; and I see no good in slaying kinsmen in battle.

32. I seek not victory, nor sovereign power, nor earthly joys. What good are sovereign power, worldly pleasures and even life to us, O Govinda?

33. Those for whom we would desire sovereign power, earthly joys and delights are here arrayed in battle, having renounced life and wealth—

34. Preceptors, sires, grandsires, sons and even grandsons, uncles, fathers-in-law, brothers-in-law, and other kinsmen.

35. These I would not kill, O Madhusudana, even though they slay me, not even for kingship of the three worlds, much less for an earthly kingdom.

36. What pleasure can there be in slaying these sons of Dhritarashtra,? Sin only can be our lot, if we slay these, usurpers though they be.

37. It does not therefore behove us to kill our kinsmen, these sons of Dhritarashtra. How may we be happy in killing our own kins?

38. Even though these, their wits warped by greed, see not the guilt that lies in destroying the family, nor the sin of treachery to comrades;

39. How can we help recoiling from this sin, seeing clearly as we do the guilt that lies in such destruction?

40. With the destruction of the family perish the eternal family virtues, and with the perishing of these virtues unrighteousness seizes the whole family.

41. When unrighteousness prevails the women of the family become corrupt, and their corruption causes a confusion of varnas.

42. This confusion verily drags the family-slayer, as well as the family, to hell, and for want of obsequial offerings and rites their departed sires fall from blessedness.

43. By the sins of these family-slayers resulting in confusion of varnas, the eternal tribal and family virtues are brought to naught.

44. For we have had it handed down to us that the men whose family virtues have been ruined are doomed to dwell in hell.

45. Alas! What a heinous sin we are about to commit, in that, from greed of the joy of sovereign power, we are prepared to slay our kith and kin!

46. Happier far would it be for me if Dhritarashtra's sons, weapons in hand, should strike me down on the battlefield, unresisting and unarmed.

Sanjaya Said:

47. Thus spake Arjuna on the field of battle, and dropping his bow and arrows sank down on his seat in the chariot, overwhelmed with anguish.

Thus ends the first discourse, entitled "Arjuna Vishada Yoga" in the converse of Lord Krishna and Arjuna, on the science of Yoga as part of the knowledge of Brahman in the Upanishad called the Bhagawadgita.

The first period of Gandhi's life is a period of twenty years, from 1894 to 1914

Discourse 2: The Theory of Sankhya and Yoga Practice

By reason of delusion, man takes wrong to be right. By reason of delusion was Arjuna led to make a difference between kinsmen and nonkinsmen.

To demonstrate that this is a vain distinction, Lord Krishna distinguishes between body (not-Self) and Atman (Self) and shows that whilst bodies are impermanent and several, Atman is permanent and one. Effort is within man's control, not the fruit thereof. All he has to do, therefore, is to decide his course of conduct or duty on each occasion and persevere in it, unconcerned about the result. Fulfillment of one's duty in the spirit of detachment or selflessness leads to Freedom.

Sanjaya Said:

1. To Arjuna, thus overcome with compassion, sorrowing, and his eyes obscured by flowing tears, Madhusudana spake these words:

The Lord Said:

2. How is it that at this perilous moment this delusion, unworthy of the noble, leading neither to heaven nor to glory, has overtaken thee?

3. Yield not to unmanliness it does not become thee. Shake off this miserable faintheartedness and arise.

* God sometimes does try to the uttermost those whom he wishes to bless.

Arjuna Said:

4.   How shall I, with arrows, engage Bhishma and Drona in battle they who are worthy of reverence?

5.   It were better far to live on alms of this world than to slay these venerable elders. Having slain them I should but have blood-stained enjoyments.

6.   Nor do we know which is better for us, that we conquer them or that they conquer us, for here stand before us Dhritarashtra's sons having killed whom we should have no desire to live.

7.   My being is paralyzed by faintheartedness; my mind discerns not duty; hence I ask thee; tell me, I pray thee, in no uncertain language, wherein lies my good. I am thy disciple; guide me; I see refuge in thee.

8.   For I see nothing that can dispel the anguish that shrivels up my senses even if I should win on earth uncontested sovereignty over a thriving kingdom or lordship over the gods.

9.   Thus spoke Gudakesha Parantapa to Hrishikesha Govinda, and with the words "I will not fight" became speechless.

10.   To him thus stricken with anguish, O Bharata! between the two armies as though mocking, addressed these words:

The Lord Said:

11.   Thou mournest for them whom thou shouldst not mourn and utterest vain words of wisdom. The wise mourn neither for the living nor for the dead.

12.   For never was I not, nor thou, nor these kings; nor will any of us cease to be hereafter.

13.   As the embodied one has, in the present body, infancy, youth and age, even so does he receive another body. The wise man is not deceived therein.

14. Contacts of the senses with their objects bring cold and heat, pleasure and pain; they come and go and are transient. Endure them.

15. O noblest of men, the wise man who is not disturbed by these, who is unmoved by pleasure and pain, he is fitted for immortality.

16. What is non-Being is never known to have been, and what is Being is never known not to have been. Of both these the secret has been seen by the seers of the Truth.

17. Know that to be imperishable whereby all this is pervaded. No one can destroy that immutable being.

18. These bodies of the embodied one who is eternal, imperishable and immeasurable are finite. Fight therefore.

19. He who thinks of This (Atman) as slayer and he who believes This to be slain, are both ignorant. This neither slays nor is ever slain.

20. This is never born nor ever dies, nor having been will ever not be any more; unborn, eternal, everlasting, ancient, This is not slain when the body is slain.

21. He who knows This to be imperishable, eternal, unborn, and immutable—whom and how can that man slay or cause to be slain?

22. As a man casts off worn-out garments and takes others that are new, even so the embodied one casts off worn-out bodies and passes on to others new.

23. This no weapons wound, This no fire burns, This no waters wet, This no wind doth dry.

24. Beyond all cutting, burning, wetting and drying is This-eternal, all-pervading, stable, immovable, everlasting.

25. Perceivable neither by the senses nor by the mind, This is called

unchangeable; therefore knowing This as such thou shouldst not grieve.

26. And if thou deemest This to be always coming to birth and always dying, even then thou shouldst not grieve.

27. For certain is the death of the born, and certain is the birth of the dead; therefore what is unavoidable thou shouldst not regret.

28. The state of all beings before birth is unmanifest; their middle state manifest; their state after death is again unmanifest. What occasion is there for lament?

29. One looks upon This as a marvel; another speaks of This as such; another hears thereof as a marvel; yet having heard This none truly knows This.

30. This embodied one in the body of every being is ever beyond all harm; thou shouldst not, therefore, grieve for any one.

Thus far Lord Krishna, by force of argument based on pure reason, has demonstrated that Atman is abiding while the physical body is fleeting, and has explained that if, under certain circumstances, the destruction of a physical body is deemed justifiable, it is delusion to imagine that the Kauravas should not be slain because they are kinsmen. Now he reminds Arjuna of the duty of a Kshatriya.

31. Again, seeing thine own duty thou shouldst not shrink from it; for there is no higher good for a Kshatriya than a righteous war.

32. Such a fight, coming unsought, as a gateway to heaven thrown open, falls only to the lot of happy Kshatriyas.

33. But if thou wilt not fight this righteous fight, then failing in thy duty and losing thine honor thou wilt incur sin.

34. The world will for ever recount the story of thy disgrace; and for a man of honor disgrace is worse than death.

35.   The Maharathas will think that fear made thee retire from battle; and thou wilt fall in the esteem of those very ones who have held thee high.

36.   Thine enemies will deride thy prowess and speak many unspeakable words about thee. What can be more painful than that?

37.   Slain, thou shalt gain heaven; victorious, thou shall inherit the earth: therefore arise, determined to fight.

Having declared the highest truth, viz. the immortality of the eternal Atman and the fleeting nature of the physical body (11–30), Krishna reminds Arjuna that a Kshatriya may not flinch from a fight which comes unsought (31–32). He then (33–37) shows how the highest truth and the performance of duty incidentally coincide with expediency. Next he proceeds to foreshadow the central teaching of the Gita in the following shloka.

38.   Hold alike pleasure and pain, gain and loss, victory and defeat, and gird up thy loins for the fight; so doing thou shalt not incur sin.

39.   Thus have I set before thee the attitude of Knowledge; hear now the attitude of Action; resorting to this attitude thou shalt cast off the bondage of action.

40.   Here no effort undertaken is lost, no disaster befalls. Even a little of this righteous course delivers one from great fear.

41.   The attitude, in this matter, springing, as it does, from fixed resolve is but one but for those who have no fixed resolve the attitudes are many-branched and unending.

When the attitude ceases to be one and undivided and becomes many and divided, it ceases to be one settled will, and is broken up into various wills of desires between which man is tossed about.

42–44. The ignorant, reveling in the letter of the Vedas, declare that there is naught else; carnally-minded, holding heaven to be their goal, they utter swelling words which promise birth as the fruit of action and which dwell on the many and varied rites to be performed for the sake of pleasure and power; intent, as they are, on pleasure and power their swelling words rob them of their wits, and they have no settled attitude which can be centered on the supreme goal.

The Vedic ritual, as opposed to the doctrine of Yoga laid down in the Gita, is alluded to here. The Vedic ritual lays countless ceremonies and rites with a view to attaining merit and heaven. These, divorced as they are from the essence of the Vedas and short-lived in their result, are worthless.

45.   The Vedas have as their domain the three gunas; eschew them, O Arjuna. Free thyself from the pairs of opposites, abide in eternal truth, scorn to gain or guard anything, remain the master of thy soul.

46.   To the extent that a well is of use when there is a flood of water on all sides, to the same extent are all the Vedas of use to an enlightened Brahmana.

47.   Action alone is thy province, never the fruits thereof; let not thy motive be the fruit of action, nor shouldst thou desire to avoid action.

48.   Act without attachment, steadfast in Yoga, even-minded in success and failure. Even-mindedness is Yoga.

49.   For action is far inferior to unattached action; seek refuge in the attitude of detached action. Pitiable are those who make fruit their motive.

50.   Here in this world a man gifted with that attitude of detachment escapes the fruit of both good and evil deeds. Gird thyself up for Yoga, therefore. Yoga is skill in action.

51.   For sages, gifted with the attitude of detachment, who renounce the fruit of action, are released from the bondage of birth and attain to the state which is free from all ills.

52.   When thy understanding will have passed through the slough of delusion, then wilt thou be indifferent alike to what thou hast heard and wilt hear.

53.   When thy understanding, distracted by much hearing, will rest steadfast and unmoved in concentration, then wilt thou attain Yoga.

Arjuna Said:

54.   What, O Keshava, is the mark of the man whose understanding is secure, whose mind is fixed in concentration? How does he talk? How sit? How move.

The Lord Said:

55.   When a man puts away, all the cravings that arise in the mind and finds comfort for himself only from Atman, then he is called the man of secure understanding.

To find comfort for oneself from Atman means to look to the spirit within for spiritual comfort, not to outside objects which in their very nature must give pleasure as well as pain. Spiritual comfort or bliss must be distinguished from pleasure or happiness. The pleasure I may derive from the possession of wealth, for instance, is delusive; real spiritual comfort or bliss can be attained only if I rise superior to every temptation even though troubled by the pangs of poverty and hunger.

56.   Whose mind is untroubled in sorrows and longeth not for joys, who is free from passion, fear and wrath—he is called the ascetic of secure understanding.

57.   Who owns attachment nowhere, who feels neither joy nor resentment whether good or bad comes his way—that man's understanding is secure.

58.   And when, like the tortoise drawing in its limbs from every side, this man draws in his senses from their objects, his understanding is secure.

59.   When a man starves his senses, the objects of those senses disappear from him, but not the yearning for them; the yearning too departs when he beholds the Supreme.

The shloka does not rule out fasting and other forms of self-restraint, but indicates their limitations, these restraints are needed for subduing the desire for sense-objects, which however is rooted out only when one has a vision of the Supreme. The higher yearning conquers all the lower yearnings.

60.   For, in spite of the wise man's endeavor, the unruly senses distract his mind perforce.

61.   Holding all these in check, the yogi should sit intent on Me; for he whose senses are under control is secure of understanding.

This means that without devotion and the consequent grace of God, man's endeavor is vain.

62.   In a man brooding on objects of the senses, attachment to them springs up; attachment begets craving and craving begets wrath.

Craving cannot but lead to resentment, for it is unending and unsatisfied.

63.   Wrath breeds stupefaction, stupefaction leads to loss of memory, loss of memory ruins the reason, and the ruin of reason spells utter destruction.

64.   But the disciplined soul, moving among sense objects with the senses weaned from likes and dislikes and brought under the control of Atman, attains peace of mind.

65.   Peace of mind means the end to all ills, for the understanding of him whose mind is at peace stands secure.

66.   The undisciplined man has neither understanding nor devotion; for him who has no devotion there is no peace, and for him who has no peace whence happiness?

67.   For when his mind runs after any of the roaming senses, it sweeps away his understanding, as the wind a vessel upon the waters.

68.   Therefore he whose senses are reined in on all sides from their objects, is the man of secure understanding.

69.   When it is night for all other beings, the disciplined soul is awake; when all other beings are awake, it is night for the seeing ascetic.

This verse indicates the divergent paths of the discipline ascetic and sensual man. Whereas the ascetic is dead to the things of the world and lives in God, the sensual man is alive only to the things of the world and dead to the things of the spirit.

70.   He in whom all longings subside, even as the waters subside in the ocean which, though ever being filled by them, never overflows—that man finds peace; not he who cherishes longing.

71.   The man who sheds all longing and moves without concern, free from the sense of "I" and "Mine"—he attains peace.

72.   This is the state, of the man who rests in Brahman; having attained to it, he is not deluded. He who abides in this state even at the hour of death passes into oneness with Brahman.

Thus ends the second discourse, entitled "Sankhya Yoga" in the converse of Lord Krishna and Arjuna, on the science of Yoga as part of the knowledge of Brahman in the Upanishad called the Bhagawadgita.

He lived in South Africa from 1893 to 1914.

Discourse 3: Karma Yoga—the Method of Work

This discourse may be said to be the key to the essence of the Gita. It makes absolutely clear the spirit and the nature of right action and shows how true knowledge must express itself in acts of selfless service.

Arjuna Said:

1.   If thou holdest that the attitude of detachment is superior to action, then why dost thou urge me to dreadful action?

2.   Thou dost seem to confuse my understanding with perplexing speech; tell me, therefore, in no uncertain voice, that alone whereby I may attain salvation.

      Arjuna is sore perplexed, for whilst on the one hand he is rebuked for his faintheartedness, on the other he seems to be advised to refrain from action (II. 49–50). But this, in reality, is not the case as the following shlokas will show.

The Lord Said:

3.   I have spoken, before, O sinless one, of two attitudes in this world—the Sankhayas', that of Jnana yoga and the Yogins', that of karma yoga.

* When I admire the wonders of a sunset or the beauty of the moon, my soul expands in the worship of the creator.

4.   Never does man enjoy freedom from action by not undertaking action, nor does he attain that freedom by mere renunciation of action.

"Freedom from action" is freedom from the bondage of action. This freedom is not to be gained by cessation of all activity, apart from the fact that this cessation is in the very nature of things impossible (see following shloka). How then may it be gained? The following shlokas will explain.

5.   For none ever remains inactive even for a moment; for all are compelled to action by the gunas inherent in prakriti.

6.   He who curbs the organs of action but allows the mind to dwell on the sense-objects — such a one, wholly deluded, is called a hypocrite.

The man who curbs his tongue but mentally swears at another is a hypocrite. But that does not mean that free rein should be given to the organs of action so long as the mind cannot be brought under control. Self-imposed physical restraint is a condition precedent to mental restraint. Physical restraint should be entirely self-imposed and not super-imposed from outside, e.g., by fear. The hypocrite who is held up to contempt here is not the humble aspirant after self-restraint. The shloka has reference to the man who curbs the body because he cannot help it while indulging the mind, and who would indulge the body too if he possibly could. The next shloka puts the thing conversely.

7.   But he, O Arjuna, who keeping all the senses under control of the mind, engages the organs in Karma yoga, without attachment-that man excels.

The mind and body should be made to accord well. Even with the mind kept in control, the body will be active in one way or another. But he whose mind is truly restrained will, for instance, close his ears to foul talk and open them only to listen to the praise of God or of good men. He will have no relish for sensual pleasures and will keep himself occupied with such activity as ennobles the soul. That is the path of action. Karma yoga is the yoga (means) which will deliver the self from the bondage of the body, and in it there is no room for self-indulgence.

41

8.   Do thou thy allotted task; for action is superior to inaction; with inaction even life's normal course is not possible.

9.   This world of men suffers bondage from all action save that which is done for the sake of sacrifice; to this end, O Kaunteya, perform action without attachment.

      "Action for the sake of sacrifice" means acts of selfless service dedicated to God.

10.   Together with sacrifice did the Lord of beings create, of old, mankind, declaring:

      "By this shall ye increase; may this be to you the giver of all your desires."

11.   "With this may you cherish the gods and may the gods cherish you; thus cherishing one another may you attain the highest good."

12.   "Cherished with sacrifice, the gods will bestow on you the desired boons." He who enjoys their gifts without rendering aught unto them is verily a thief.

      "Gods" in shlokas 11 and 12 must be taken to mean the whole creation of God. The service of all created beings is the service of the gods and the same is sacrifice.

13.   The righteous men who eat the residue of the sacrifice are freed from all sin, but the wicked who cook for themselves eat sin.

14.   From food springs all life, from rain is born food; from sacrifice comes rain and sacrifice is the result of action.

15.   Know that action springs from Brahman and Brahman from the Imperishable; hence the all-pervading Brahman is ever firm-founded on sacrifice.

16.   He who does not follow the wheel thus set in motion here below, he, living in sin, sating his senses, lives in vain.

17. But the man who revels in Atman, who is content in Atman and who is satisfied only with Atman, for him no action exists.

18. He has no interest whatever in anything done, nor in anything not done, nor has he need to rely on anything for personal ends.

19. Therefore, do thou ever perform without attachment the work that thou must do; for performing action without attachment man attains the Supreme.

20. For through action alone Janaka and others achieved perfection; even with a view to the guidance of mankind thou must act.

21. Whatever the best man does, is also done by other men, what example he sets, the world follows.

22. For me there is naught to do in the three worlds, nothing worth gaining that I have not gained; yet I am ever in action.

An objection is sometimes raised that God being impersonal is not likely to perform any physical activity, at best He may be supposed to act mentally. This is not correct. For the unceasing movement of the sun, the moon, the earth etc. signifies God in action. This is not mental but physical activity. Though God is without form and impersonal, He acts as though He had form and body. Hence though He is ever in action, He is free from action, unaffected by action. What must be borne in mind is that, just as all Nature's movements and processes are mechanical and yet guided by Divine Intelligence or Will, even so man must reduce his daily conduct to mechanical regularity and precision, but he must do so intelligently. Man's merit lies in observing divine guidance at the back of these processes and in an intelligent imitation of it rather than in emphasizing the mechanical nature thereof and reducing himself to an automation. One has but to withdraw the self, withdraw attachment to fruit from all action, and then not only mechanical precision but security from all wear and tear will be ensured. Acting thus man remains fresh until the end of his days. His body will perish in due course, but his soul will remain evergreen without a crease or a wrinkle.

23.   Indeed, for were I not, unslumbering, ever to remain in action men would follow my example in every way.

24.   If I were not to perform my task, these worlds would be ruined; I should be the same cause of chaos and of the end of all mankind.

Chapter 53

25.   Just as, with attachment, the unenlightened perform all actions, even so, but unattached, should the enlightened man act, with a desire for the welfare of humanity.

26.   The enlightened may not confuse the mind of the unenlightened, who are attached to action; rather must he perform all actions unattached, and thus encourage them to do likewise.

27.   All action is entirely done by the gunas of prakriti. Man, deluded by the sense of "I," thinks, "I am the doer."

28.   But he who understands the truth of the various gunas and their various activities, knows that it is the gunas that operate on the gunas; he does not claim to be the doer.

As breathing, winking and similar processes are automatic and man claims no agency for them, he being conscious of the processes only when disease or similar cause arrests them, in a similar manner all his acclivities should be automatic, without his arrogating to himself the agency or responsibility thereof. A man of charity does not even know that he is doing charitable acts, it is his nature to do so, he cannot help it. This detachment can only come from tireless endeavor and God's grace.

29.   Deluded by the gunas of prakriti men become attached to the activities of the gunas; he who knows the truth of things should not unhinge the slow-witted who have not the knowledge.

30.   Cast all thy acts on Me, with thy mind fixed on the indwelling Atman, and without any thought of fruit, or sense of "mine" shake off thy fever and fight!

He who knows the Atman inhabiting the body and realizes Him to be a part of the supreme Atman will dedicate everything to Him, even as a faithful servant acts as a mere shadow of his master and dedicates to him all that he does. For the master is the real doer, the servant but the instrument.

31. Those who always act according to the rule I have here laid down, in faith and without caviling—they too are released from the bondage of their actions.

32. But those who cavil at the rule and refuse to conform to it are fools, dead to all knowledge; know that they are lost.

33. Even a man of knowledge acts according to his nature; all creatures follow their nature; what then will constraint avail?

This does not run counter to the teaching in II. 61 and II. 68. Self-restraint is the means of salvation (VI. 35; XIII. 7). Man's energies should be bent toward achieving complete self-restraint until the end of his days. But if he does not succeed, neither will constraint help him. The shloka does not rule out restraint but explains that nature prevails. He who justifies himself saying, "I cannot do this, it is not in my nature," misreads the shloka. True we do not know our nature, but habit is not nature. Progress, not decline, ascent, not descent, is the nature of the soul, and therefore every threatened decline or descent ought to be resisted. The next verse makes this abundantly clear.

34. Each sense has its settled likes and dislikes toward its objects; man should not come under the sway of these, for they are his besetters.

Hearing, for instance, is the object of the ears which may be inclined to hear something and disinclined to hear something else. Man may not allow himself to be swayed by these likes and dislikes, but must decide for himself what is conducive to his growth, his ultimate end being to reach the state beyond happiness and misery.

35. Better one's own duty, bereft of merit, than another's well-performed; better is death in the discharge of one's duty; another's duty is fraught with danger.

One man's duty may be to serve the community by working as a sweeper, another's may be to work as an accountant. An accountant's work may be more inviting, but that need not draw the sweeper away from his work. Should he allow himself to be drawn away he would himself be lost and put the community into danger. Before God the work of man will be judged by the spirit in which it is done, not by the nature of the work which makes no difference whatsoever. Whoever acts in a spirit of dedication fits himself for salvation.

Arjuna Said:

36.   Then what impels man to sin, even against his will, as though by force compelled?

The Lord Said:

37.   It is Lust, it is Wrath, born of the guna-Rajas. It is the arch-devourer, the arch-sinner. Know this to be man's enemy here.

38.   As fire is obscured by smoke, a mirror by dirt, and the embryo by the amnion, so is knowledge obscured by this.

39.   Knowledge is obscured by this eternal enemy of the wise man, in the form of Lust, the insatiable fire.

40.   The senses, the mind and the reason are said to be its great seat; by means of these it obscures knowledge and stupefies man.

When Lust seizes the senses, the mind is corrupted, discrimination is obscured and reason ruined. See II. 62–64.

41.   Therefore bridle thou first the senses and then rid thyself of this sinner, the destroyer of knowledge and discrimination.

42.   Subtle, they say, are the senses; subtler than the senses is the mind; subtler than the mind is the reason; but subtler even than the reason is He.

43.   Thus realizing Him to be subtler than the reason, and controlling the self by the Self (Atman), destroy, O Mahabahu, this enemy-Lust, so hard to overcome.

When man realizes Him, his mind will be under his control, not swayed by the senses. And when the mind is conquered, what power has Lust? It is indeed a subtle enemy, but when once the senses, the mind and the reason are under the control of the subtlemost Self, Lust is extinguished.

Thus ends the third discourse entitled "Karma Yoga" in the converse of Lord Krishna and Arjuna, on the science of Yoga, as part of the knowledge of Brahman in the Upanishad called the Bhagawadgita.

Man and Wife : **Mohandas and Kasturba**
Picture taken in 1915 upon Gandhi's return
to India

Discourse 4: The Yoga of Knowledge and Renunciation of Work

This discourse further explains the subject-matter of the third and describes the various kinds of sacrifice.

The Lord Said:

1.   I expounded this imperishable yoga to Vivasvat; Vivasvat communicated it to Manu, and Manu to Ikshvaku.

2.   Thus handed down in succession, the royal sages learnt it; with long lapse of time it dwindled away in this world, O Parantapa.

3.   The same ancient yoga have I expounded to thee today; for thou art My devotee and My friend, and this is the supreme mystery.

Arjuna Said:

4.   Later was Thy birth, my Lord, earlier that of Vivasvat. How then am I to understand that Thou didst expound it in the beginning?

The Lord Said:

5.   Many births have we passed through, O Arjuna, both thou and I; I know them all, thou knowest them not.

*Happiness is when what you think, what you say, and what you do are in harmony.

6.   Though unborn and inexhaustible in My essence, though Lord of all beings, yet assuming control over My Nature, I come into being by My mysterious power.

7.   For whenever Right declines and Wrong prevails, then O Bharata, I come to birth.

8.   To save the righteous, to destroy the wicked, and to reestablish Right I am born from age to age.

Here is comfort for the faithful and affirmation of the truth that Right ever prevails. An eternal conflict between Right and Wrong goes on. Sometimes the latter seems to get the upper hand, but it is Right which ultimately prevails. The good are never destroyed, for Right —which is Truth —cannot perish; the wicked are destroyed, because Wrong has no independent existence. Knowing this let man cease to arrogate to himself authorship and eschew untruth, violence and evil. Inscrutable Providence —the unique power of the Lord —is ever at work. This in fact is avatara, incarnation. Strictly speaking there can be no birth for God.

9.   He who knows the secret of this My divine birth and action is not born again, after leaving the body; he comes to Me.

For when a man is secure in the faith that Right always prevails, he never swerves therefrom, pursuing to the bitterest end and against serious odds, and as no part of the effort proceeds from his ego, but all is dedicated to Him, being ever one with Him, he is released from birth to death.

10.   Freed from passion, fear and wrath, filled full with Me, relying on Me, and refined by the fiery ordeal of knowledge, many have become one with Me.

11.   In whatever way men resort to Me, even so do I render to them. In every way the path men follow is Mine.

That is, the whole world is under His ordinance. No one may break God's law with impunity. As we sow, so shall we reap. This law operates inexorably without fear or favor.

12. Those who desire their actions to bear fruit worship the gods here; for in this world of men the fruit of action is quickly obtainable.

Gods, as indicated before, must not be taken to mean the heavenly beings of tradition, but whatever reflects the divine. In that sense man is also a god. Steam, electricity and the other great forces of Nature are all gods.

Propitiation of these forces quickly bears fruit, as we well know, but it is short-lived. It fails to bring comfort to the soul and it certainly does not take one even a short step toward salvation.

13. The order of the four varnas was created by Me according to the different gunas and karma of each; yet know that though, therefore, author thereof, being changeless I am not the author.

14. Actions do not affect Me, nor am I concerned with the fruits thereof. He who recognizes Me as such is not bound by actions.

For man has thus before him the supreme example of one who though in action is not the doer thereof. And when we are but instruments in His hands, where then is the room for arrogating responsibility for action?

15. Knowing this did men of old, desirous of freedom, perform action; do thou, then, just as they did—the men of old in days gone by.

16. "What is action? What is inaction?"—here even the wise are perplexed. I will then expound to thee that action knowing which thou shalt be saved from evil.

17. For it is meet to know the meaning of action, of forbidden action, as also inaction. Impenetrable is the secret of action.

18. Who sees action in action and action in inaction, he is enlightened among men, he is a yogi, he has done all he need do.

The "action" of him who, though ever active, does not claim to be the doer, is inaction; and the "inaction" of him who, though outwardly avoiding action, is always building castles in his own mind, is action. The enlightened man who has grasped the secret of action knows that no action proceeds from him, all proceeds from God and hence he selflessly remains absorbed in action. He is the true yogi. The man who acts self-fully misses the secret of action and cannot distinguish between Right and Wrong. The soul's natural progress is toward selflessness and purity and one might, therefore, say that the man who strays from the path of purity strays from selflessness. All actions of the selfless man are naturally pure.

19.   He whose every undertaking is free from desire and selfish purpose, and he who has burnt all his actions in the fire of knowledge—such a one the wise call a pandita.

20.   He who has renounced attachment to the fruit of action, who is ever content, and free from all dependence, he, though immersed in action, yet acts not.

That is, his action does not bind him.

21.   Expecting naught, holding his mind and body in check, putting away every possession, and going through action only in the body he incurs no stain.

The purest act, if tainted by "self," binds. But when it is done in a spirit of dedication, it ceases to bind. When "self" has completely subsided, it is only the body that works. For instance, in the case of a man who is asleep his body alone is working. A prisoner doing his prison tasks has surrendered his body to the prison authorities and only his body, therefore, works. Similarly, he who has voluntarily made himself God's prisoner, does nothing himself. His body mechanically acts, the doer is God, hot he. He has reduced himself to nothingness.

22.   Content with whatever chance may bring, rid of the pairs of opposites, free from ill-will, even-minded in success and failure, he is not bound though he acts.

23.   Of the free soul who has shred all attachment, whose mind is firmly grounded in knowledge, who acts only for sacrifice, all karma is extinguished.

24.   The offering of sacrifice is Brahman; the oblation is Brahman; it is offered by Brahman in the fire that is Brahman; thus he whose mind is fixed on acts dedicated to Brahman must needs pass on to Brahman.

25.   Some yogins perform sacrifice in the form of worship of the gods, others offer sacrifice of sacrifice itself in the fire that is Brahman.

26.   Some offer as sacrifice the sense of hearing and the other senses in the fires of restraint; others sacrifice sound and the other objects of sense in the fires of the senses.

The restraint of the senses—hearing and others—is one thing; and directing them only to legitimate objects, e.g., listening to hymns in the praise of god, is another, although ultimately both amount to the same thing.

27.   Others again sacrifice all the activities of the senses and of the vital energy in the yogic fire of self-control kindled by knowledge.

That is to say, they lose themselves in the contemplation of the Supreme.

28.   Some sacrifice with material gifts; with austerities; with yoga; some with the acquiring and some with the imparting of knowledge. All these are sacrifices of stern vows and serious endeavor.

29.   Others absorbed in the practices of the control of the vital energy sacrifice the outward in the inward and the inward in the outward, or check the flow of both the inward and the outward vital airs.

The reference here is to the three kinds of practices of the control of vital energy—puraka, rechaka, and kumbhaka.

30.   Yet others, abstemious in food, sacrifice one form of vital energy in another. All these know what sacrifice is and purge themselves of all impurities by sacrifice.

31.   Those who partake of the residue of sacrifice—called amrita (ambrosia) —attain to everlasting Brahman. Even this world is not for a non-sacrificer; how then the next?

32.   Even so various sacrifices have been described in the Vedas; know them all to proceed from action; knowing this thou shalt be released.

Action here means mental, physical and spiritual action. No sacrifice is possible without this triple action and no salvation without sacrifice. To know this and to put the knowledge into practice is to know the secret of sacrifice. In fine, unless man uses all his physical, mental and spiritual gifts in the service of mankind, he is a thief unfit for Freedom. He who uses his intellect only and spares his body is not a full sacrificer. Unless the mind and the body and the soul are made to work in unison, they cannot be adequately used for the service of mankind. Physical, mental and spiritual purity is essential for the harmonious working. Therefore man should concentrate on developing, purifying, and turning to the best of all his faculties.

33.   Knowledge-sacrifice is better than material sacrifice, for all action which does not bind finds its consummation in Knowledge (jnana).

Who does not know that works of charity performed without knowledge often result in great harm? Unless every act, however noble its motive, is informed with knowledge, it lacks perfection. Hence the complete fulfillment of all action is in knowledge.

34.   The masters of knowledge who have seen the Truth will impart to thee this Knowledge; learn it through humble homage and service and by repeated questioning.

The three conditions of knowledge—homage, repeated questioning and service—deserve to be carefully borne in mind in this age. Homage or obeisance means humility and service is a necessary accompaniment; else it would be mock homage. Repeated questioning is equally essential, for without a keen spirit of inquiry, there is no knowledge. All this presupposes devotion to and faith in the person approached. There can be no humility, much less service, without faith.

35. When thou hast gained this knowledge thou shalt not again fall into such error; by virtue of it thou shalt see all beings without exception in thyself and thus in Me.

The adage "Yatha pinde tatha brahmande" — "as with the self so with the universe" — means the same thing. He who has attained Self-realization sees no difference between himself and others.

36. Even though thou be the most sinful of sinners, thou shalt cross the ocean of sin by the boat of knowledge.

37. As a blazing fire turns its fuel to ashes, O Arjuna, even so the fire of Knowledge turns all actions to ashes.

38. There is nothing in this world so purifying as Knowledge. He who is perfected by yoga finds it in himself in the fullness of time.

39. It is the man of faith who gains knowledge—the man who is intent on it and who has mastery over his senses; having gained knowledge, he comes ere long to the supreme peace.

40. But the man of doubt, without knowledge and without faith, is lost; for him who is given to doubt there is neither this world nor that beyond, nor happiness.

41. He who has renounced all action by means of yoga, who has severed all doubt by means of knowledge—him self-possessed, no actions bind, O Dhananjaya!

42. Therefore, with the sword of Self-realization sever thou this doubt, bred of ignorance, which has crept into thy heart! Betake thyself to yoga and arise!

Thus ends the fourth discourse, entitled "Jnana—Karma—Sannyasa—Yoga" in the converse of Lord Krishna and Arjuna, on the science of Yoga, as part of the knowledge of Brahman in the Upanishad called the Bhagawadgita.

During the satyagraha
struggle, 1914

Discourse 5: The Yoga of Renunciation of Work

This discourse is devoted to showing that renunciation of action as such is impossible without the discipline of selfless action and that both are ultimately one.

Arjuna Said:

1.   Thou laudest renunciation of actions, O Krishna, whilst at the same time thou laudest performance of action; tell me for a certainty which is the better.

The Lord Said:

2.   Renunciation and performance of action both lead to salvation; but of the two, karmayoga (performance) is better than sannyasa (renunciation).

3.   Him one should know as ever renouncing who has no dislikes and likes; for he who is free from the pairs of opposites is easily released from bondage.

   That is, not renunciation of action but of attachment to the pairs determines true renunciation. A man who is always in action may be a good sannyasa (renouncer) and another who may be doing no work may well be a hypocrite. See III. 6.

* *If we are to teach real peace in this world, and if we are to carry on a real war against war, we shall have to begin with the children*

4.   It is the ignorant who speak of sankhya and yoga as different,
        not so those who have knowledge. He who is rightly established
        even in one wins to the fruit of both.

        *The yogi engrossed in sankhya (knowledge) lives even in thought for the
        good of the world and attains the fruit of karmayoga by the sheer power
        of his thought. The karmayogi ever engrossed in unattached action
        naturally enjoys the peace of the jnanayogi.*

5.   The goal that the sankhyas attain is also reached by the yogins.
        He sees truly who sees both sankhya and yoga as one.

6.   But renunciation, O Mahabahu, is hard to attain except by
        yoga; the ascetic equipped with yoga attains Brahman ere long.

7.   The yogi who has cleared himself, has gained mastery over his
        mind and all his senses, who has become one with the Atman
        in all creation, although he acts he remains unaffected.

8.   The yogi who has seen the Truth knows that it is not he that
        acts whilst seeing, hearing, touching, smelling, eating, walking,
        sleeping, or breathing.

9.   Talking, letting go, holding fast, opening or closing the eyes-in
        the conviction that is the senses that are moving in their
        respective spheres.

        *So long as "self" endures, this detachment cannot be achieved. A sensual
        man therefore may not shelter himself under the pretence that it is not he
        but his senses that are acting. Such a mischievous interpretation betrays
        a gross ignorance of the Gita and right conduct. The next shloka makes
        this clear.*

10.   He who dedicates his actions to Brahman and performs them
        without attachment is not smeared by sin, as the lotus-leaf by
        water.

11.   Only with the body, mind and intellect and also with the senses,
        do the yogins perform action without attachment for the sake
        of self-purification.

12. A man of yoga obtains everlasting peace by abandoning the fruit of action; the man ignorant of yoga, selfishly attached to fruit, remains bound.

13. Renouncing with the mind all actions, the dweller in the body, who is master of himself, rests happily in his city of nine gates, neither doing nor getting anything done.

The principal gates of the body are the two eyes, the two nostrils, the two ears, the mouth, and the two organs of excretion — though really speaking the countless pores of the skin are no less gates. If the gatekeeper always remains on the alert and performs his task, letting in or out only the objects that deserve ingress or egress, then of him it can truly be said that he has no part in the ingress or egress, but that he is a passive witness. He thus does nothing nor gets any thing done.

14. The Lord creates neither agency nor action for the world; neither does he connect action with its fruit. It is nature that is at work.

God is no doer. The inexorable law of karma prevails, and in the very fulfillment of the law — giving everyone his deserts, making everyone reap what he sows — lies God's abounding mercy and justice. In undiluted justice is mercy. Mercy which is inconsistent with justice is not mercy but its opposite. But man is not a judge knowing past, present, and future. So for him the law is reversed and mercy or forgiveness is the purest justice. Being himself ever liable to be judged he must accord to others what he would accord to himself, viz. forgiveness. Only by cultivating the spirit of forgiveness can he reach the state of a yogi, whom no actions bind, the man of even-mindedness, the man skilled in action.

15. The Lord does not take upon Himself anyone's vice or virtue; it is ignorance that veils knowledge and deludes all creatures.

The delusion lies in man arrogating to himself the authorship of action and the attributing to God the consequences thereof — punishment or reward as the case may be.

16. But to them whose ignorance is destroyed by the knowledge of Atman, this their knowledge, like the sun, reveals the Supreme.

17. Those whose intellect is suffused with That, whose self has become one with That, who abide in That, and whose end and aim is that, wipe out their sins with knowledge, and go whence there is no return.

18. The men of Self-realization look with an equal eye on a brahmana possessed of learning and humility, a cow, an elephant, a dog and even a dog-eater.

That is to say, they serve every one of them alike, according to the needs of each. Treating a brahmana and shwapaka (dog-eater) alike means that the wise man will suck the poison off a snake-bitten shwapaka with as much eagerness and readiness as he would from a snake-bitten brahmana.

19. In this very body they have conquered the round of birth and death, whose mind is anchored in sameness; for perfect Brahman is same to all, therefore in Brahman they rest.

As a man thinks, so he becomes, and therefore those whose minds are bent on being the same to all achieve that sameness and become one with Brahman.

20. He whose understanding is secure, who is undeluded, who knows Brahman and who rests in Brahman, will neither be glad to get what is pleasant, nor sad to get what is unpleasant.

21. He who has detached himself from contacts without, finds bliss in Atman; having achieved union with Brahman he enjoys eternal bliss.

He who has weaned himself from outward objects to the inner Atman is fitted for union with Brahman and the highest bliss. To withdraw oneself from contacts without and to bask in the sunshine of union with Brahman are two aspects of the same state, two sides of the same coin.

22. For the joys derived from sense-contacts are nothing but mines of misery; they have beginning and end the wise man does not revel therein.

23.   The man who is able even here on earth, ere he is released from the body, to hold out against the floodtide of lust and wrath,- he is a yogi, he is happy.

As a corpse has no likes and dislikes, no sensibility to pleasure and pain, even so he who though alive is dead to these, he truly lives, he is truly happy.

24.   He who finds happiness only within, rest only within, light only within—that yogi, having become one with nature, attains to oneness with Brahman.

25.   They win oneness with Brahman—the seers whose sins are wiped out, whose doubts are resolved, who have mastered themselves, and who are engrossed in the welfare of all beings.

26.   Rid of lust and wrath, masters of themselves, the ascetics who have realized Atman find oneness with Brahman everywhere around them.

27–28. That ascetic is ever free—who, having shut out the outward sense-contacts, sits with his gaze fixed between the brows, outward and inward breathing in the nostrils made equal; his senses, mind, and reason held in check; rid of longing, fear and wrath; and intent on Freedom.

These shlokas refer to some of the yogic practices laid down in the Yoga-sutras. A word of caution is necessary regarding these practices. They serve for the yogin the same purpose as athletics and gymnastics do for the bhogin (who pursues worldly pleasures). His physical exercises help the latter to keep his senses of enjoyment in full vigor. The yogic practices help the yogin to keep his body in condition and his senses in subjection. Men versed in these practices are rare in these days, and few of them turn them to good account. He who has achieved the preliminary stage on the path to self-discipline, he who has a passion for Freedom, and who having rid himself of the pairs of opposites has conquered fear, would do well to go in for these practices which will surely help him. It is such a disciplined man alone who can, through these practices, render his body a holy temple of God. Purity both of the mind and body is a sine qua non, without which these processes are likely, in the first instance, to lead a man astray and then drive him deeper into the slough of delusion. That this has been the result in some cases many know from actual experience. That is why that prince of yogins, Patanjali gave the first place to yamas (cardinal vows) and niyamas (casual vows), and held as eligible for yogic practices only those who have gone through the preliminary discipline.

The five cardinal vows are: non-violence, truth, non-stealing, celibacy, non-possession.

The five casual vows are: bodily purity, contentment, the study of the scriptures, austerity, and meditation of God.

29. Knowing Me as the Acceptor of sacrifice and austerity, the great Lord of all the worlds, the Friend of all creation, the yogi attains to peace.

This shloka may appear to be in conflict with shlokas 14 and 15 of this discourse and similar ones in other discourses. It is not really so.

Almighty God is Doer and non-Doer, Enjoyer and non-Enjoyer both. He is indescribably, beyond the power of human speech. Man somehow strives to have a glimpse of Him and in so doing invests Him with diverse and even contradictory attributes.

Thus ends the fifth discourse, entitled "Sannyasa Yoga" in the converse of Lord Krishna and Arjuna, on the science of Yoga, as part of the knowledge of Brahman, in the Upanishad called the Bhagawadgita.

Gandhi at thirty-nine.

Discourse 6: The Yoga of Self-Control

This discourse deals with some of the means for the accomplishment of Yoga or the discipline of the mind and its activities.

The Lord Said:

1. He who performs all obligatory action, without depending on the fruit thereof, is a sannyasin and a yogin—not the man who neglects the sacrificial fire nor he who neglects action.

    Fire here may be taken to mean all possible instruments of action. Fire was needed when sacrifices used to be performed with its help. Assuming that spinning were a means of universal service in this age, a man by neglecting the spinning wheel would not become a sannyasi.

2. What is called sannyasa, know thou to be yoga for none can become a yogin who has not renounced selfish purpose.

3. For the man who seeks to scale the heights of yoga, action is said to be the means; for the same man, when he has scaled those heights, repose is said to be the means.

    He who has purged himself of all impurities and who has achieved even-mindedness will easily achieve Self-realization. But this does not mean that he who has scaled the heights of yoga will disdain to work for the

---

* I look only to the good qualities of men. Not being faultless myself, I won't presume to probe into the faults of others.

guidance of the world. On the contrary that work will be to him not only the breath of his nostrils, but also as natural to him as breathing. He will do so by the sheer force of will. See V. 4.

4. When a man is not attached either to the objects of sense or to actions and sheds all selfish purpose, then he is said to have scaled the heights of yoga.

5. By one's Self should one raise oneself, and not allow oneself to fall; for Atman (Self) alone is the friend of self, and Self alone is self's foe.

6. His Self alone is friend, who has conquered himself by his Self: but to him who has not conquered himself and is thus inimical to himself, even his Self behaves as foe.

7. Of him who has conquered himself and who rests in perfect calm the self is completely composed, in cold and heat, in pleasure and pain, in honor and dishonor.

8. The yogin who is filled with the contentment of wisdom and discriminative knowledge, who is firm as a rock, who has mastered his senses, and to whom a clod of earth, a stone and gold are the same, is possessed of yoga.

9. He excels who regards alike the boon companion, the friend, the enemy, the stranger, the mediator, the alien and the ally, as also the saint and the sinner.

Chapter 88

10. Let the yogi constantly apply his thought to Atman remaining alone in a scheduled place, his mind and body in control, rid of desires and possessions.

11.   Fixing for himself, in a pure spot, a firm seat, neither too high nor yet too low, covered with kusha grass, thereon a deerskin, and thereon a cloth;

12.   Sitting on that seat, with mind concentrated, the functions of thought and sense of control, he should set himself to the practice of yoga for the sake of self-purification.

13.   Keeping himself steady, holding the trunk, the neck and the head in a straight line and motionless, fixing his eye on the tip of his nose, and looking not around.

14.   Tranquil in spirit, free from fear, steadfast in the vow of brahmacharya, holding his mind in control, the yogi should sit, with all his thoughts on Me, absorbed in Me.

       Brahmacharya (usually translated "celibacy") means not only sexual continence but observance of all the cardinal vows for the attainment of Brahman.

15.   The yogi, who ever thus, with mind controlled, unites himself to Atman, wins the peace which culminates in Nirvana, the peace that is in Me.

16.   Yoga is not for him who eats too much, nor for him who fasts too much, neither for him who sleeps too much, nor yet for him who is too wakeful.

17.   To him who is disciplined in food and recreation, in effort in all activities, and in sleep and waking, yoga (discipline) becomes a relief from all ills.

18.   When one's thought, completely controlled, rests steadily on only Atman, when one is free from longing for all objects of desire, then one is called a yogin.

19.   As a taper in a windless spot flickers not, even so is a yogin, with his thought controlled, seeking to unite himself with Atman.

20. Where thought curbed by the practice of yoga completely ceases, where a man sits content within himself, Atman having seen Atman;

21. Where he experiences that endless bliss beyond the senses which can be grasped by reason alone; wherein established he swerves not from the Truth;

22. Where he holds no other gain greater than that which he has gained; and where, securely seated, he is not shaken by any calamity however great;

23. That state should be known as yoga (union with the Supreme), the disunion from all union with pain. This yoga must one practice with firm resolve and unwearying zeal.

24. Shaking oneself completely free from longings born of selfish purpose; reining in the whole host of senses, from all sides, with the mind itself;

25. With reason held securely by the will, he should gradually attain calm and with the mind established in Atman think of nothing.

26. Wherever the fickle and unsteady mind wanders, thence should it be reined and brought under the sole sway of Atman.

28. The yogin, cleansed of all stain, unites himself ever thus to Atman, easily enjoys the endless bliss of contact with Brahman.

29. The man equipped with yoga looks on all with an impartial eye, seeing Atman in all beings and all beings in Atman.

30. He who sees Me everywhere and everything in Me, never vanishes from Me nor I from him.

31. The yogin who, anchored in unity, worships Me abiding in all beings, lives and moves in me, no matter how he live and move.

So long as "self" subsists, the Supreme Self is absent; when "self" is extinguished, the Supreme Self is seen everywhere. Also see note on XIII. 23.

32. He who, by likening himself with others, senses pleasure and pain equally for all as for himself, is deemed to be the highest yogi.

Arjuna Said:

33. I do not see how this yoga, based on the equal-mindedness that Thou hast expounded to me, can steadily endure, because of fickleness (of the mind).

34. For fickle is the mind unruly, overpowering and stubborn; to curb it is, I think, as hard as to curb the wind.

The Lord Said:

35. Undoubtedly the mind is fickle and hard to curb; yet it can be held in check by constant practice and dispassion.

36. Without self-restraint, yoga, I hold, is difficult to attain; but the self-governed soul can attain it by proper means, if he strives for it.

Arjuna Said:

37. If one, possessed of faith, but slack of effort, because of his mind straying from yoga, reach not perfection in yoga, what end does he come to?

38. Without a foothold, and floundering in the path to Brahman fallen from both, is he indeed not lost like a dissipated cloud?

39. This my doubt, O Krishna, do thou dispel utterly; for there is to be found none other than thou to banish this doubt.

The Lord Said:

40. Neither in this world, nor in the next, can there be ruin for him no well-doer, oh loved one, meets with a sad end.

41. Fallen from yoga, a man attains the worlds of righteous souls, and having dwelt there for numberless years is then born in a house of pure and gentle blood.

42. Or he may even be born into a family of yogins, though such birth as this is all too rare in this world.

43. There he discovers the intellectual stage he had reached in previous birth, and thence he stretches forward again toward perfection.

44. By virtue of that previous practice he is borne on, whether he will it or not, even he with a desire to know yoga passes beyond the Vedic ritual.

45. But the yogi who perseveres in his striving, cleansed of sin, perfected through many births, reaches the highest state.

46. The yogin is deemed higher than the man of austerities; he is deemed also higher than the man of knowledge; higher is he than the man engrossed in ritual; therefore be thou a yogin.

47. And among all yogins, he who worships Me with faith, his inmost self all rapt in Me, is deemed by me to be the best yogin.

Thus ends the sixth discourse entitled "Dhyana Yoga" in the converse of Lord Krishna and Arjuna, on the science of Yoga, as part of the knowledge of Brahman in the Upanishad called the Bhagawadgita.

Gandhi (center) with colleagues at his Law Office, South Africa, 1913

Discourse 7: The Yoga of Wisdom and Knowledge

With this discourse begins an exposition of the nature of Reality and the secret of devotion.

The Lord Said:

1. Hear how, with thy mind riveted on me, by practicing yoga and making me the sole refuge, thou shalt, without doubt, know me fully.

2. I will declare to thee, in its entirety, this knowledge, combined with discriminative knowledge, which when thou hast known there remains here nothing more to be known.

3. Among thousands of men hardly one strives after perfection; among those who strive hardly one knows Me in truth.

4. Earth, Water, Fire, Air, Ether, Mind, Reason and Ego-thus eightfold is my prakriti divided.

   The eightfold prakriti is substantially the same as the field described in XIII. 5 and the perishable Being in XV. 16.

5. This is My lower aspect; but know thou My other aspect, the higher—which is Jiva (the Vital Essence) by which this world is sustained.

* There is a sufficiency in the world for man's need but not for man's greed.

67

6.   Know that these two compose the source from which all beings spring; I am the origin and end of the entire universe.

7.   There is nothing higher than I; all this is strung on Me as a row of gems upon a thread.

8.   In water I am the savor; in the sun and the moon I am the light; the syllable AUM in all the Vedas; the sound in ether, and manliness in men.

9.   I am the sweet fragrance in earth; the brilliance in fire; the life in all beings; and the austerity in ascetics.

10.   Know Me to be the primeval seed of all beings; I am the reason of rational beings and the splendor of the splendid.

11.   Of the strong, I am the strength, divorced from lust and passion; in beings I am desire undivorced from righteousness.

12.   Know that all the manifestations of the three gunas, sattva, rajas, and tamas, proceed from none but Me; yet I am not in them; they are in Me.

      God is not dependent on them, they are dependent on Him. Without Him those various manifestations would be impossible.

13.   Befogged by these manifestations of the three gunas, the entire world fails to recognize Me, the imperishable, as transcending them.

14.   For this My divine delusive mystery made up of the three gunas is hard to pierce; but those who make Me their sole refuge pierce the veil.

15.   The deluded evil-doers, lowest of men, do not see refuge in Me; for, by reason of this delusive mystery, they are bereft of knowledge and given to devilish ways.

16.   Four types of well-doers are devoted to Me; they are, the afflicted, the spiritual seeker, the material seeker, and the enlightened.

17. Of these the enlightened, ever attached to Me in single-minded devotion, is the best; for to the enlightened I am exceedingly dear and he is dear to Me.

18. All these are estimable indeed, but the enlightened I hold to be My very self; for he, the true yogi, is stayed on Me alone, the supreme goal.

19. At the end of many births the enlightened man finds refuge in Me; rare indeed is this great soul to whom "Vasudeva is all."

20. Men, bereft of knowledge by reason of various longings, seek refuge in other gods, pinning their faith on diverse rites, guided by their own nature.

21. Whatever form one desires to worship in faith and devotion, in that very form I make that faith of his secure.

22. Possessed of that faith he seeks a propitiate that one, and obtains there through his longings, dispensed in truth by none but Me.

23. But limited is the fruit that falls to those shortsighted ones; those who worship the gods go to the gods, those who worship Me come unto Me.

24. Not knowing My transcendent, imperishable, supreme character, the undiscerning think Me who am unmanifest to have become manifest.

25. Veiled by the delusive mystery created by My unique power, I am not manifest to all; this bewildered world does not recognize Me, birthless and changeless.

     Having the power to create this world of sense and yet unaffected by it, He is described as having unique power.

26. I know all creatures past, present and to be; but no one knows Me.

27. All creatures in this universe are bewildered, by virtue of the delusion of the pairs of opposite sprung from likes and dislikes.

28. But those virtuous men whose sin has come to an end, freed from delusion and of the pairs of opposites, worship Me in steadfast faith.

29. Those who endeavor for freedom from age and death by taking refuge in Me, know in full that Brahman, Adhyatma and all Karma.

30. Those who know Me, including Adhibhuta, Adhidaiva, Adhiyajna, possessed of even-mindedness, they know Me even at the time of passing away.

The terms in italics are defined in the next discourse the subject of which is indicated in 29–30. The sense is that every nook and cranny of the universe is filled with Brahman, that He is the sole Agent of all action, and that the man who imbued to Him, becomes one with Him at the time of passing hence. All his desires are extinguished in his vision of Him and he wins his freedom.

Thus ends the seventh discourse, entitled "Jananvijnana Yoga" in the converse of Lord Krishna and Arjuna, on the science of Yoga, as part of the knowledge of Brahman in the Upanishad called the Bhagawadgita.

A young boy leads
Gandhiji for a walk

Discourse 8: The Imperishable Supreme

The nature of the Supreme is further expounded in this discourse.

Arjuna Said:

1. What is that Brahman? What is Adhyatma? What Karma, O Purushottama? What is called Adhibhuta? And what Adhidaiva?

2. And who here in this body is Adhiyajna and how? And how at the time of death art Thou to be known by the self-controlled?

The Lord Said:

3. The Supreme, the Imperishable is Brahman; its manifestation is Adhyatma; the creative process whereby all beings are created is called Karma.

4. Adhibhuta is My perishable form; Adhidaivata is the individual self in that form; and O best among the embodied, Adhiyajna am I in this body, purified by sacrifice.

---

* It has always been a mystery to me how men can feel themselves honored by the humiliation of their fellow beings.

That is, from Imperishable Unmanifest down to the perishable atom everything in the universe is the Supreme and an expression of the Supreme. Why then should mortal man arrogate to himself authorship of anything rather than do His bidding and dedicate all action to Him?

5.   And he who, at the last hour remembering Me only, departs leaving the body, enters into Me; of that there is no doubt.

6.   Or whatever form a man continually contemplates, that same he remembers in the hour of death, and to that very form he goes.

7.   Therefore at all times remember Me and fight on; thy mind and reason thus on Me fixed thou shalt surely come to Me.

8.   With thought steadied by constant practice, and wandering nowhere, he who meditates on the Supreme Celestial Being, goes to Him.

9–10.   Whoso, at the time of death, with unwavering mind, with devotion, and fixing the breath rightly between the brows by the power of yoga, meditates on the Sage, the Ancient, the Ruler, subtler than the subtlest, the Supporter of all, the Inconceivable, glorious as the sun beyond the darkness—he goes to that Supreme Celestial Being.

11.   That which the knowers of the Vedas call the Imperishable (or that word which the knowers of the Vedas repeat), wherein the ascetics freed from passion enter and desiring which they practice brahmacharya, that Goal (or Word) I will declare to thee in brief.

12.   Closing all the gates, locking up the mind in the hridaya, fixing his breath within the head, rapt in yogic meditation;

13.   Whoso departs leaving the body uttering AUM—Brahman in one syllable—repeatedly thinking on Me, he reaches the highest state.

14.   That yogi easily wins to Me who, ever attached to Me, constantly remembers Me with undivided mind.

15. Great souls, having come to Me, reach the highest perfection; they come not again to birth, unlasting and (withal) an abode of misery.

16. From the world of Brahma down, all the worlds are subject to return, but on coming to Me there is no rebirth.

17. Those men indeed know what is Day and what is Night, who know that Brahma's day lasts a thousand yugas and that his night too is a thousand yugas long.

That is to say, our day and night of a dozen hours each are less than the infinitesimal fraction of a moment in that vast cycle of time. Pleasures pursued during these incalculably small moments are as illusory as a mirage. Rather than waste these brief moments, we should devote them to serving God through service of mankind. On the other hand, our time is such a small drop in the ocean of eternity that if we fail of our object here, viz. Self-realization, we need not despair. She should bide our time.

18. At the coming of Day all the manifest spring forth from the Unmanifest, and at the coming of Night they are dissolved into that same Unmanifest.

Knowing this too, man should understand that he has very little power over things, the round of birth and death is ceaseless.

19. This same multitude of creatures come to birth, again and again; they are dissolved at the coming of Night, whether they will or not; and at the break of Day they are reborn.

20. But higher than the Unmanifest is another Unmanifest Being, everlasting, which perisheth not when all creatures perish.

21. This Unmanifest, named the Imperishable, is declared to be the highest goal. For those who reach it there is no return. That is my highest abode.

22. This Supreme Being, may be won by undivided devotion; in It all beings dwell, by It all is pervaded.

23.   Now I will tell thee, the conditions which determine the exemption from return, as also the return, of yogins after they pass away hence.

24.   Fire, Light, Day, the Bright Fortnight, the six months of the Northern Solstice—through these departing men knowing Brahman go to Brahman.

25.   Smoke, Night, the Dark Fortnight, the six months of the Southern Solstice—Therethrough the yogin attains to the lunar light and thence returns.

I do not understand the meaning of these two shlokas. They do not seem to me to be consistent with the teaching of the Gita. The Gita teaches that he whose heart is meek with devotion, who is devoted to unattached action and has seen the Truth must win salvation, no matter when he dies. These shlokas seem to run counter to this. They may perhaps be stretched to mean broadly that a man of sacrifice, a man of light, a man who has known Brahman finds release from birth if he retains that enlightenment at the time of death, and that on the contrary the man who has none of these attributes goes to the world of the moon—not at all lasting—and returns to birth. The moon, after all, shines with borrowed light.

26.   These two paths—bright and dark—are deemed to be the eternal paths of the world; by the one a man goes to return not, by the other he returns again.

The Bright one may be taken to mean the path of knowledge and the dark one that of ignorance.

27.   The Yogin knowing these two paths falls not into delusion, O Partha; therefore, at all times, O Arjuna, remain steadfast in yoga.

"Will not fall into delusion" means that he who knows the two paths and has known the secret of even-mindedness will not take the path of ignorance.

28.   Whatever fruit of good deeds is laid down as accruing from (a study of) the Vedas, from sacrifices, austerities, and acts of charity—all that the yogin transcends, on knowing this, and reaches the Supreme and Primal Abode.

He who has achieved even-mindedness by dint of devotion, knowledge and service not only obtains the fruit of all his good actions, but also wins salvation.

Thus ends the eighth discourse entitled "Brahma Yoga" in the converse of Lord Krishna and Arjuna, on the science of Yoga, as part of the knowledge of Brahman in the Upanishad called the Bhagawadgita.

Gandhi and Communism,
1934-1940

Discourse 9: The Most Secret and Sovereign Yoga of Knowledge

This discourse reveals the glory of devotion.

The Lord Said:

1. I will now declare to thee, who art uncensorious, this mysterious knowledge, together with discriminative knowledge, knowing which thou shalt be released from ill.

2. This is the king of sciences, the king of mysteries, pure and sovereign, capable of direct comprehension, the essence of dharma, easy to practice, changeless.

3. Men who have no faith in this doctrine, far from coming to Me, return repeatedly to the path of this world of death.

4. By Me, unmanifest in form, this whole world is pervaded; all beings are in Me, I am not in them.

5. And yet those beings are not in Me. That indeed is My unique power as Lord! Sustainer of all beings, I am not in them; My Self brings them into existence.

---

* *It is easy enough to be friendly to one's friends. But to befriend the one who regards himself as your enemy is the quintessence of true religion. The other is mere business.*

The sovereign power of God lies in this mystery, this miracle, that all beings are in Him and yet not in Him, He in them and yet not in them. This is the description of God in the language of mortal man. Indeed He soothes man by revealing to him all His aspects by using all kinds of paradoxes. All beings are in him inasmuch as all creation is His; but as He transcends it all, as He really is not the author of it all, it may be said with equal truth that the beings are not in Him. He really is in all His true devotees, He is not, according to them, in those who deny Him. What is this if not a mystery, a miracle of God?

6. As the mighty wind, moving everywhere, is ever contained in ether, even so know that all beings are contained in Me.

7. All beings, merge into my prakriti, at the end of a kalpa, and I send them forth again when a kalpa begins.

8. Resorting to my prakriti, I send forth again and again this multitude of beings, powerless under the sway of prakriti.

9. But all this activity, does not bind Me, seated as one indifferent, unattached to it.

10. With me as Presiding Witness, prakriti gives birth to all that moves and does not move; and because of this, the wheel of the world keeps going.

11. Not knowing My transcendent nature as the sovereign Lord of all beings, fools condemn Me incarnated as man.

    For they deny the existence of God and do Not recognize the Director in the human body.

12. Vain are the hopes, actions and knowledge of those witless ones who have resorted to the delusive nature of monsters and devils.

13. But those great souls who resort to the divine nature, know Me as the Imperishable Source of all beings and worship Me with an undivided mind.

14.   Always declaring My glory, striving in steadfast faith, they do Me devout homage; ever attached to Me, they worship Me.

15.   Yet others, with knowledge-sacrifice, worship Me, who am to be seen everywhere, as one, as different or as many.

16.   I am the sacrificial vow; I am the sacrifice; I the ancestral oblation; I the herb; I the sacred text; I the clarified butter; I the fire; I the burnt offering.

17.   Of this universe I am the Father, Mother, Creator, Grandsire: I am what is to be known, the sacred syllable AUM; the rig, the Saman and the Yajus;

18.   I am the Goal, the Sustainer, the Lord, the Witness, the Abode, the Refuge, the Friend; the Origin, the End the Preservation, the Treasurehouse, the Imperishable Seed.

19.   I give heat; I hold back and pour forth rain; I am deathlessness and also death. O Arjuna, Being and not-Being as well.

20.   Followers of the three Vedas, who drink the soma juice and are purged of sin, worship Me with sacrifice and pray for going to heaven; they reach the holy world of the gods and enjoy in heaven the divine joys of the gods.

The reference is to the sacrificial ceremonies and rites in vogue in the days of the Gita. We cannot definitely say what they were like nor what the soma juice exactly was.

21.   They enjoy the vast world of heaven, and their merit spent, they enter the world of the mortals; thus those who, following the Vedic law, long for the fruit of their action earn but the round of birth and death.

22.   As for those who worship Me, thinking on Me alone and nothing else, ever attached to Me, I bear the burden of getting them what they need.

There are thus three unmistakable marks of a true yogi or bhakta — even-mindedness, skill in action, undivided devotion. These three must be completely harmonized in a yogi. Without devotion there is no even-mindedness, without even-mindedness no devotion, and without skill in action devotion and even-minded might well be a pretense.

23. Even those who, devoted to other gods, worship them in full faith, even they, worship none but Me, though not according to the rule.

"Not according to the rule" means not knowing Me as the Impersonal and the Absolute.

24. For I am the Acceptor and the Director of all sacrifices; but not recognizing Me as I am, they go astray.

25. Those who worship the gods go to the gods; those who worship the manes go to the manes; those who worship the spirits go to the spirits; but those who worship Me come to Me.

26. Any offering of leaf, flower, fruit or water, made to Me in devotion, by an earnest soul, I lovingly accept.

That is to say, it is the Lord in every being whom we serve with devotion who accepts the service.

27. Whatever thou doest, whatever thou eatest, whatever thou offerest as sacrifice or gift, whatever austerity thou dost perform, dedicate all to Me.

28. So doing thou shalt be released from the bondage of action, yielding good and evil fruit; having accomplished both renunciation and performance, thou shalt be released (from birth and death) and come unto Me.

29. I am the same to all beings; with Me there is non-disfavored, none favored; but those who worship Me with devotion are in Me and I in them.

30.   A sinner, howsoever great, if he turns to Me with undivided
       devotion, must indeed be counted a saint; for he has a settled
       resolve.

       The undivided devotion subdues both his passions and his evil deeds.

31.   For soon he becomes righteous and wins everlasting peace;
       know for a certainty, that my bhakta never perishes.

32.   For finding refuge in Me, even those who though are born of
       the womb of sin, women, vaishyas, and shudras too, reach the
       supreme goal.

33.   How much more then, the pure brahmanas and seer-kings who
       are my devotees? Do thou worship Me, therefore, since thou
       hast come to this fleeting and joyless world.

34.   On Me fix thy mind, to Me bring thy devotion, to Me offer thy
       sacrifice, to Me make thy obeisance; thus having attached
       thyself to Me and made Me thy end and aim, to Me indeed shalt
       thou come.

       Thus ends the ninth discourse entitled "Rajavidya-rajaguhya
       Yoga" in the converse of Lord Krishna and Arjuna, on the
       science of Yoga, as part of the knowledge of Brahman in the
       Upanishad called the Bhagawadgita.

Mahatma Gandhi's bust gathering dust in South Africa

Discourse 10: I Am Everything and the Best

For the benefit of His devotees, the Lord gives in this discourse a glimpse of His divine manifestations.

The Lord Said:

1. Yet once more hear My supreme word, which I will utter to thee, gratified one, for thy benefit.

2. Neither the gods nor the great seers know My origin; for I am, every way, the origin of them both.

3. He who knows Me, the great lord of the worlds, as birthless and without beginning, he among mortals, undeluded, is released from sins.

4. Discernment, knowledge, freedom from delusion, long suffering, truth, self-restraint, inward calm, pleasure, pain, birth, death, fear and fearlessness;

5. Non-violence, even-mindedness, contentment, austerity, beneficence, good and ill fame—all these various attributes of creatures proceed verily from Me.

6. The seven great seers, the ancient four, and the Manus too were born of Me and of My mind, and of them were born all the creatures in the world.

* In prayer it is better to have a heart without words than words without a heart.

7. He who knows in truth My immanence and My yoga becomes gifted with unshakable yoga; of this there is no doubt.

8. I am the source of all, all proceeds from me; knowing this, the wise worship Me with hearts full of devotion.

9. With me in their thoughts, their whole soul devoted to Me, teaching one another, with me ever on their lips, they live in contentment and joy.

10. To these, ever in tune with Me worshipping me with affectionate devotion, I give the power of selfless action, whereby they come to Me.

11. Out of every compassion for them, I who dwell in their hearts, destroy the darkness, born of ignorance, with the refulgent lamp of knowledge.

Arjuna Said:

12. Lord! Thou art the supreme Brahman, the supreme Abode, the supreme Purifier! Everlasting Celestial Being, the Primal God, Unborn, All-pervading.

13. Thus have all the seers—the divine seer Narada, Asita, Devala, Vyasa—declared Thee; and Thou Thyself dost tell me so.

14. All that Thou tellest me is true, I know, verily, Lord, neither the gods nor the demons know Thy manifestation.

15. Thyself alone Thou knowest by Thyself, O Source and Lord of all beings, God of Gods, O Ruler of the universe.

16. Indeed Thou oughtest to tell me of all Thy manifestations, without a remainder, whereby Thou dost pervade the worlds.

17. O Yogin! constantly meditating on Thee, how am I to know Thee? In what various aspects am I to think of Thee, O Lord?

18.   Recount to me yet again, in full detail, Thy unique power and Thy immanence, For my ears cannot be sated with listening to Thy life-giving words.

The Lord Said:

19.   Yea, I will unfold to thee, My divine manifestations — the chiefest only; for there is no limit to their extent.

20.   I am the Atman, seated in the heart of every being; I am the beginning, the middle and the end of all beings.

21.   Of the Adityas I am Vishnu; of luminaries, the radiant Sun; of Maruts, I am Marichi; of constellations, the moon.

22.   Of the Vedas I am the Sama Veda; of the gods Indra; of the senses I am the mind; of beings I am the consciousness.

23.   Of Rudras I am Shankara; of Yakshas and Rakshasas Kubera; of Vasus I am the Fire; of mountains Meru.

24.   Of priests, know Me to be the chief Brihaspati; of army captains I am Kartikeya; and of waters the ocean.

25.   Of the great seers I am Bhrigu; of words I am the one syllable "AUM;" of sacrifices I am the Japa sacrifice; of things immovable, the Himalaya.

26.   Of all trees I am Ashvattha; of the divine seers, Narada; of the heavenly choir I am Chitraratha; of the perfected I am Kapila the ascetic.

27.   Of horses, Know Me to be the Uchchaihshravas born with Amrita; of mighty elephants I am Airavata; of men, the monarch.

28.   Of weapons, I am Vajra; of cows, Kamadhenu; I am Kandarpa, the God of generation; of serpents I am Vasuki.

29.   Of cobras I am Anata; of water-dwellers I am Varuna; of the manes I am Aryaman; and of the chastisers, Yama.

30.   Of demons I am Prahlada; of reckoners, the time; of beasts I am the lion; and of birds, Garuda.

31.   Of cleansing agents I am the Wind; of wielders of weapons, Rama; of fishes I am the crocodile; of rivers the Ganges.

32.   Of creations I am the beginning, end and middle, O Arjuna; of sciences, the science of spiritual knowledge; of debators, the right argument.

33.   Of letters, the letter A; of compounds I am the dvandva; I am the imperishable Time; I am the creator to be seen everywhere.

34.   All-seizing Death am I, as the source of things to be; in feminine virtues I am Kirti (glory), Shri (beauty), Vak (speech), Smriti (memory), Medha (intelligence), Dhriti (constancy) and Kshama (forgiveness).

35.   Of Saman hymns I am Brihat Saman; of metres, Gayatri; of months I am Margashirsha; of seasons, the spring.

36.   Of deceivers I am the dice-play; of the splendid the splendor; I am victory, I am resolution, I am the goodness of the good.

The "dice-play of deceivers" need not alarm one. For the good and evil nature of things is not the matter in question, it is the directing and immanent power of God that is being described. Let the deceivers also know that they are under God's rule and judgment and put away their pride and deceit.

37.   Of Vrishnis I am Vasudeva; of Pandavas Dhananjaya; of ascetics I am Vyasa; and of seers, Ushanas.

38.   I am the rod of those that punish; the strategy of those seeking victory; of secret things I am silence, and the knowledge of those that know.

39.   Whatever is the seed of every being, O Arjuna, that am I; there is nothing, whether moving or fixed, that can be without Me.

40.   There is no end to my divine manifestations; what extent of them I have told thee now is only by way of illustration.

41.   Whatever is glorious, beautiful and mighty know thou that all such has issued from a fragment of My splendor.

42.   But why needest thou to learn this at great length? With but a part of Myself I stand upholding this universe.

Thus ends the tenth discourse, entitled "Vibhuti Yoga" in the converse of Lord Krishna and Arjuna, on the science of Yoga, as part of the knowledge of Brahman, in the Upanishad called the Bhagawadgita.

A rare studio photograph of Gandhi taken in London at the request of Lord Irwin, 1931.

Discourse 11: Behold My Cosmic Form

In this discourse, the Lord reveals to Arjuna's vision what Arjuna has heard with his ears — the Universal Form of the Lord. This discourse is a favorite with the Bhaktas. Here there is no argument, there is pure poetry. Its solemn music [1] reverberates in one's ears and it is not possible to tire of reading it again and again.

Arjuna Said:

1. Out of Thy grace toward me, thou hast told me the supreme mystery revealing the knowledge of the Supreme; it has banished my delusion.

2. Of the origin and destruction of beings I have heard from Thee in full detail, as also Thy imperishable ajesty [sic]!

3. Thou art indeed as Thou hast described Thyself! I do crave to behold, now, that form of Thine as Ishvara.

4. If, Lord, thou thinkest it possible for me to bear the sight, reveal to me, Thy imperishable form.

The Lord Said:

5. Behold, my forms divine in their hundreds and thousands, infinitely diverse, infinitely various in color and aspect.

---

* There is nothing that wastes the body like worry, and one who has any faith in God should be ashamed to worry about anything whatsoever.

6.   Behold the Adityas, the Vasus, the Rudras, the two Ashwins, the Maruts; behold, O Bharata, numerous marvels never revealed before.

7.   Behold today, in my body, the whole universe, moving and unmoving, all in one, and whatever else thou cravest to see.

8.   But thou canst not see Me with these thine own eyes. I give thee the eye divine; behold My sovereign power!

Sanjaya Said:

9.   With these words, the great Lord of Yoga, Hari, then revealed to Partha His supreme form as Ishvara.

10.   With many mouths and many eyes, many wondrous aspects, many divine ornaments, and many brandished weapons divine.

11.   Wearing divine garlands and vestments, anointed with divine perfumes, it was the form of God, all-marvelous [sic], infinite, seen everywhere.

12.   Were the splendor of a thousand suns to shoot forth all at once in the sky that might perchance resemble the splendor of that Mighty One.

13.   Then did Pandava see the whole universe in its manifold divisions gathered as one in the body of that God of gods.

14.   Then Dhananjaya, wonderstruck and thrilled in every fiber of his being, bowed low his head before the Lord, addressing Him thus with folded hands.

Arjuna Said:

15.   With Thy form, O Lord, I see all the gods and the diverse multitudes of beings, the Lord Brahma, on his lotus-throne and all the seers and serpents divine.

16.   With many arms and bellies, mouths and eyes, I see Thy infinite form everywhere. Neither Thy end, nor middle, nor beginning, do I see, O Lord of the Universe, Universal-formed!

17.   With crown and mace and disc, a mass of effulgence, gleaming everywhere I see Thee, so dazzling to the sight, bright with the splendor of the fiery sun blazing from all sides — incomprehensible.

18.   Thou art the Supreme Imperishable worthy to be known; Thou art the final resting place of this universe; Thou art the changeless guardian of the Eternal Dharma; Thou art, I believe, the Everlasting Being.

19.   Thou hast no beginning, middle nor end; infinite is Thy might; arms innumerable; for eyes, the sun and the moon; Thy mouth a blazing fire, overpowering the universe with Thy radiance.

20.   By Thee alone are filled the spaces between heaven and earth and all the quarters; at the sight of this Thy wondrous terrible form, the three worlds are sore oppressed!

21.   Here, too, the multitudes of gods are seen to enter Thee; some awe-struck praise Thee with folded arms; the hosts of great seers and siddhas, "All Hail" on their lips, hymn Thee with songs of praise.

22.   The Rudras, Adityas, Vasus, Sadhyas, all the gods, the twin Ashwins, Maruts, Manes, the hosts of Gandharvas, Yakshas, Asuras and Siddhas — all gaze on Thee in wonderment.

23.   At the sight of thy mighty form, many-mouthed, with eyes, arms, thighs and feet innumerable, with many vast bellies, terrible with many jaws, the worlds feel fearfully oppressed, and so do I.

24.   For as I behold Thee touching the sky, glowing, numerous-hued with gaping mouths and wide resplendent eyes, I feel oppressed in my innermost being; no peace nor quiet I find, O Vishnu!

25. As I see Thy mouths with fearful jaws, resembling the Fire of Doom, I lose all sense of direction, and find no relief. Be gracious.

26. All the sons of Dhritarashtra, and with them the crowd of kings, Bhishma, Drona, and that Karna too, as also our chief warriors—

27. Are hastening into the fearful jaws of Thy terrible mouths. Some indeed, caught between Thy teeth, are seen, their heads being crushed to atoms.

28. As rivers, in their numerous torrents, run headlong to the sea, even so the heroes of the world of men rush into Thy flaming mouths.

29. As moths, fast-flying, plunge into blazing fire, straight to their doom, even so these rush headlong into Thy mouths, to their destruction.

30. Devouring all these from all sides, Thou lappest them with Thy flaming tongues; Thy fierce rays blaze forth, filling the whole universe with their luster.

31. Tell me, Lord, who Thou art so dread of form! Hail to Thee, Be gracious! I desire to know Thee, Primal Lord; for I comprehend not what Thou dost.

The Lord Said:

32. Doom am I, full-ripe, dealing death to the worlds, engaged in devouring mankind. Even without slaying them not one of the warriors, ranged for battle against thee, shall survive.

33. Therefore, do thou arise, and win renown! Defeat thy foes and enjoy a thriving kingdom. By Me have these already been destroyed; be thou no more than an instrument!

34. Drona, Bhishma, Jayadratha and Karna, as also the other warrior chiefs—already slain by Meslay thou! Fight! Victory is thine over the foes in the field.

Sanjaya Said:

35. Hearing this world of Keshava, crown-wearer Arjuna folded his hands, and trembling made obeisance. Bowing and all hesitant, in faltering accents, he proceeded to address Krishna once more.

Arjuna Said:

36. Right proper it is, that Thy praise should stir the world to gladness and tender emotion; the Rakshasas in fear fly to every quarter and all the hosts of Siddhas do reverent homage.

37. And why should they not bow down to Thee, O Mahatma? Thou art the First Creator, greater even than Brahma. O Ananta, O Devesha, O Jagannivasa, Thou art the Imperishable, Being, not-Being, and That which transcends even these.

38. Thou art the Primal God, the Ancient Being; Thou art the Final Resting Place of this Universe; Thou art the Knower, the "to-beknown," the Supreme Abode; by Thee, O Myriad-formed, is the universe pervaded.

39. Thou art Vayu, Yama, Agni, Varuna, Shashanka, Prajapati, and Prapitamaha! All Hail to Thee, a thousand times all hail! Again and yet again all hail to Thee!

40. All hail to Thee from before and behind! All hail to Thee from every side, O All; Thy prowess is infinite, Thy might is measureless! Thou holdest all; therefore Thou art all.

41. If ever in carelessness, thinking of Thee as comrade, I addressed Thee saying, "O Krishna!", "O Yadava!" not knowing Thy greatness, in negligence or in affection,

42. If ever I have been rude to Thee in jest, whilst at play, at rest-time, or at meals, whilst alone or in company, O Achyuta, forgive Thou my fault—I beg of Thee, O Incomprehensible!

43. Thou art Father of this world, of the moving and the un-moving; thou art its adored, its worthiest, Master; there is none equal to Thee; how then any greater than Thee? Thy power is matchless in the three worlds.

44. Therefore, I prostrate myself before Thee, and beseech Thy grace, O Lord adorable! As father with son, as comrade with comrade, so shouldst Thou bear, beloved Lord, with me, Thy loved one.

45. I am filled with joy to see what never was seen before, and yet my heart is oppressed with fear. Show me that original form of Thine, O Lord! Be gracious.

46. I crave to see Thee even as Thou wast, with crown, with mace, and disc in hand; wear Thou, once more, that four-armed form, O thousand-armed Vishvamurti!

The Lord Said:

47. It is to favor thee, O Arjuna, that I have revealed to thee, by My own unique power, this My form Supreme, Resplendent, Universal, Infinite, Primal—which none save thee has ever seen.

48. Not by the study of the Vedas, not by sacrifice, not by the study of other scriptures, not by gifts, nor yet by performance of rites or of fierce austerities can I, in such a form, be seen by any one save thee in the world of men!

49. Be thou neither oppressed nor bewildered to look on this awful form of Mine. Banish thy fear, ease thy mind, and lo! behold Me once again as I was.

Sanjaya Said:

50. So said Vasudeva to Arjuna, and revealed to him once more His original form. Wearing again His form benign, the Mahatma consoled him terrified.

Arjuna Said:

51.   Beholding again thy benign human form I am come to myself and once more in my normal state.

The Lord Said:

52.   Very hard to behold is that form of Mine which thou hast seen; even the gods always yearn to see it.

53.   Not by the Vedas, not by penance, nor by gifts, nor yet by sacrifice, can any behold Me in the form that thou hast seen.

54.   But by single-minded devotion, I may in this form be known and seen, and truly entered into.

55.   He alone comes to me, who does My work, who has made Me his goal, who is My devotee, who has renounced attachment, who has ill-will toward none.

Thus ends the eleventh discourse, entitled "Vishvarupadarshana Yoga" in the converse of Lord Krishna and Arjuna, on the science of Yoga as part of the knowledge of Brahman in the Upanishad called the Bhagawadgita.

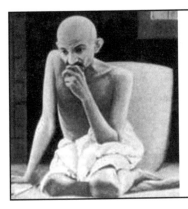

Non cooperation with evil is as much a duty as is cooperation with good.

Discourse 12: The Yoga of Devotion and Contemplation

Thus we see that vision of God is possible only through single-minded devotion. Contents of devotion must follow as a matter of course. This twelfth discourse should be learnt by heart even if all discourses are not. It is one of the shortest. The marks of a devotee should be carefully noted.

Arjuna Said:

1.   Of the devotees who thus worship Thee, incessantly attached, and those who worship the Imperishable Unmanifest, which are the better yogins?

The Lord Said:

2.   Those I regard as the best yogins who, riveting their minds on Me, ever attached, worship Me, with the highest faith.

3.   But those who worship the Imperishable, the indefinable, the Unmanifest, the Omnipresent, the Unthinkable, the Rock-seated, the Immovable, the Unchanging,

4.   Keeping the whole host of senses in complete control, looking on all with an impartial eye, engrossed in the welfare of all beings—these come indeed to Me.

5.   Greater is the travail of those whose mind is fixed on the Unmanifest; for it is hard for embodied mortals to gain the Unmanifest-Goal.

* To give service to a single heart by a single act is better than a thousand heads bowing in prayer.

Mortal man can only imagine the Unmanifest, the Impersonal, and as his language fails him he often negatively describes It as "Neti," "Neti" (Not That, Not That). And so even iconoclasts are at bottom no better than idol-worshippers. To worship a book, to go to church, or to pray with one's face in a particular direction—all these are forms of worshipping the Formless in an image or idol. And yet, both the idol-breaker and the idol-worshipper cannot lose sight of the fact that there is something which is beyond all form, Unthinkable, Formless, Impersonal, Changeless. The highest goal of the devotee is to become one with the object of his devotion. The bhakta extinguishes himself and merges into, becomes, Bhagvan. This state can best be reached by devoting oneself to some form, and so it is said that the short cut to the Unmanifest is really the longest and the most difficult.

6.   But those who casting all their actions on Me, making Me their all in all, worship Me with the meditation of undivided devotion,

7.   Of such, whose thoughts are centered on Me, I become ere long the Deliverer from the ocean of this world of death.

8.   On Me set thy mind, on Me rest thy conviction; thus without doubt shalt thou remain only in Me hereafter.

9.   If thou canst not set thy mind steadily on Me, then by the method of constant practice seek to win Me.

10.   If thou art also unequal to this method of constant practice, concentrate on service for Me; even thus serving Me thou shalt attain perfection.

11.   If thou art unable even to do this, then dedicating all to Me, with mind controlled, abandon the fruit of action.

12.   Better is knowledge than practice, better than knowledge is concentration, better than concentration is renunciation of the fruit of all action, from which directly issues peace.

"Practice" (abhyasa) is the practice of the yoga of meditation and control of psychic processes; "knowledge" (jnana) is intellectual effort; "concentration" (dhyana) is devoted worship. If as a result of all this there is no renunciation of the fruit of action, "practice" is no "practice," "knowledge" is no "knowledge," and "concentration" is no "concentration."

13. Who has ill-will toward none, who is friendly and compassionate, who has shed all thought of "mine" or "I," who regards pain and pleasure alike, who is long-suffering;

14. Who is ever content, gifted with yoga, self-restrained, of firm conviction, who has dedicated his mind and reason to Me— that devotee (bhakta) of Mine is dear to Me.

15. Who gives no trouble to the world, to whom the world causes no trouble, who is free from exultation, resentment, fear and vexation—that man is dear to Me.

16. Who expects naught, who is pure, resourceful, unconcerned, untroubled, who indulges in no undertakings—that devotee of Mine is dear to Me.

17. Who rejoices not, neither frets nor grieves, who covets not, who abandons both good and ill—that devotee of Mine is dear to Me.

18. Who is same to foe and friend, who regards alike respect and disrespect, cold and heat, pleasure and pain, who is free from attachment;

19. Who weighs in equal scale blame and praise, who is silent, content with whatever his lot, who owns no home, who is of steady mind—that devotee of Mine is dear to Me.

20. They who follow this essence of dharma, as I have told it, with faith, keeping Me as their goal—those devotees are exceeding dear to Me.

Thus ends the twelfth discourse entitled "Bhakti Yoga" in the converse of Lord Krishna and Arjuna, on the science of Yoga, as part of the knowledge of Brahman in the Upanishad called the Bhagawadgita.

How would Gandhi lead the leaderless?

Discourse 13: The Field and Its Knower

This discourse treats of the distinction between the body (not-Self) and the Atman (the Self).

The Lord Said:

1. This body, is called the Field; he who knows it is called the knower of the Field by those who know.

2. And understand Me to be, the knower of the Field in all the Fields; and the knowledge of the Field and the knower of the Field, I hold, is true knowledge.

3. What the Field is, what its nature, what its modifications, and whence is what, as also who He is, and what His power—hear this briefly from Me.

4. This subject has been sung by seers distinctively and in various ways, in different hymns as also in aphoristic texts about Brahman well reasoned and unequivocal.

5. The great elements, Individuation, Reason, the Unmanifest, the ten senses, and the one (mind), and the five spheres of the senses;

6. Desire, dislike, pleasure, pain, association, consciousness, cohesion—this, in sum, is what is called the Field with its modifications.

* You must not lose faith in humanity. Humanity is an ocean; if a few drops of the ocean are dirty, the ocean does not become dirty.

The great elements are Earth, Water, Fire, Air and Ether. "Individuation" is the thought of I, or that the body is "I;" the "Unmanifest" is prakriti or maya; the ten senses are the five senses of perception — smell, taste, sight, touch and hearing, and the five organs of action, viz.: the hands, the feet, the tongue, and the two organs of excretion. The five spheres or objects of the senses are smell, savor, form, touch, and sound. "Association" is the property of the different organs to cooperate. Dhriti is not patience or constancy but cohesion, i.e., the property of all the atoms in the body to hold together; from "individuation" springs this cohesion. Individuation is inherent in the unmanifest prakriti. The undeluded man is he who can cast off the individuation or ego, and having done so the shock of an inevitable thing like death and pairs of opposites caused by sense-contacts fail to affect him. The Field, subject to all its modifications, has to be abandoned in the end by the enlightened and the unenlightened alike.

7. Freedom from pride and pretentiousness, nonviolence, forgiveness, uprightness, service of the Master, purity, steadfastness, self-restraint;

8. Aversion from sense-objects, absence of conceit, realization of the painfulness and evil of birth, death, age and disease;

9. Absence of attachment, refusal to be wrapped up in one's children, wife, home and family, even-mindedness whether good or ill befall;

10. Unwavering and all-exclusive devotion to Me, resort to secluded spots, distaste for the haunts of men;

11. Settled conviction of the nature of the Atman, perception of the goal of the knowledge of Truth—all this is declared to be Knowledge and the reverse of it is ignorance.

12. I will (now) expound to thee that which is to be known and knowing which one enjoys immortality; it is the supreme Brahman which has no beginning, which is called neither Being nor non-Being.

The Supreme can be described neither as Being nor as non-Being. It is beyond definition or description, above all attributes.

13.   Everywhere having hands and feet, everywhere having eyes, heads, mouths, everywhere having ears, It abides embracing everything in the universe.

14.   Seeming to possess the functions of the senses, It is devoid of all the senses; It touches naught, upholds all; having no gunas, It experiences the gunas.

15.   Without all beings, yet within; immovable yet moving, so subtle that It cannot be perceived; so far and yet so near It is. He who knows It is within It, close to It; mobility and immobility, peace and restlessness, we owe to It, for It has motion and yet is motionless.

16.   Undivided, It seems to subsist divided in all beings; this Brahman—That which is to be known as the Sustainer of all, yet It is their Devourer and Creator.

17.   Light of all lights, It is said to be beyond darkness; It is knowledge, the object of knowledge, to be gained only by knowledge; It is seated in the hearts of all.

18.   Thus have I expounded in brief the Field, Knowledge and That which is to be known; My devotee, when he knows this, is worthy to become one with Me.

19.   Know that Prakriti and Purusha are both without beginning; know that all the modifications and gunas are born of Prakriti.

20.   Prakriti is described as the cause in the creation of effects from causes; Purusha is described as the cause of the experiencing of pleasure and pain.

21.   For the Purusha, residing in Prakriti, experiences the gunas born in Prakriti; attachment to these gunas is the cause of his birth in good or evil wombs. Prakriti in common parlance is Maya. Purusha is the Jiva. Jiva acting in accordance with his nature experiences the fruit of actions arising out of the three gunas.

22.   What is called in this body the Witness, the Assentor, the Sustainer, the Experiencer, the Great Lord and also the Supreme Atman, is Supreme Being.

23.   He who thus knows Purusha and Prakriti with its gunas, is not born again, no matter how he live and move.

Read in the light of discourses II, IX and XII this shloka may not be taken to support any kind of libertinism. It shows the virtue of self-surrender and selfless devotion. All actions bind the self, but if all are dedicated to the Lord they do not bind, rather they release him.

He who has thus extinguished the "self" or the thought of "I" and who acts as ever in the great witness' eye, will never sin nor err. The self-sense is at the root of all error or sin. Where the "I" has been extinguished, there is no sin. This shloka shows how to steer clear of all sin.

24.   Some through meditation hold the Atman by themselves in their own self; others by Sankhya Yoga, and others by Karma Yoga.

25.   Yet others, not knowing (Him) thus, worship (Him) having heard from others; they too pass beyond death, because of devoted adherence to what they have heard.

26.   Wherever something is born, animate or inanimate, know thou Bharatarshabha, that it issues from the union of the Field and the Knower of the Field.

27.   Who sees abiding in all beings the same Parameshvara, imperishable in the perishable, he sees indeed.

28.   When he sees the same Ishvara abiding everywhere alike, he does not hurt himself by himself and hence he attains the highest goal.

He who sees the same God everywhere merges in Him and sees naught else; he thus does not yield to passion, does not become his own foe and thus attains Freedom.

29. Who sees that it is Prakriti that performs all actions and thus (knows) that Atman performs them not, he sees indeed.

Just as, in the case of a man who is asleep, his "Self" is not the agent of sleep, but Prakriti, even so the enlightened man will detach his "Self" from all activities. to the pure everything is pure. Prakriti is not unchaste, it is when arrogant man takes her as wife that of these twain passion is born.

30. When he sees the diversity of beings as founded in unity and the whole expanse issuing therefrom, then he attains to Brahman.

To realize that everything rests in Brahman is to attain to the state of Brahman. Then Jiva becomes Shiva.

31. This imperishable Supreme Atman, though residing in the body, acts not and is not stained, for he has no beginning and no gunas.

32. As the all-pervading ether, by reason of its subtlety, is not soiled even so Atman pervading every part of the body is not soiled.

33. As the one Sun illumines the whole universe, even so the Master of the Field illumines the whole field!

34. Those who, with the eyes of knowledge, thus perceive the distinction between the Field and the Knower of the Field, and (the secret) of the release O beings from Prakriti, they attain to the Supreme.

Thus ends the thirteenth discourse, entitled "Kshetra-kshetrajnavibhaga Yoga" in the converse of Lord Krishna and Arjuna, on the science of Yoga, as part of the knowledge of Brahman in the Upanishad called the Bhagawadgita.

Gandhi outside of his house on the Sevagram ashram, which he founded in Maharashtra in 1936.

Discourse 14: The Three Basic Kinds

The description of Prakriti naturally leads on to that of its constituents, the Gunas, which form the subject of this discourse. And that, in turn, leads to a description of the marks of him who has passed beyond the three gunas. These are practically the same as those of the man of secure understanding (II. 54–72) as also those of the ideal Bhakta (XII. 12–20).

The Lord Said:

1. Yet again I will expound the highest and the best of all knowledge, knowing which all the sages passed hence to the highest perfection.

2. By having recourse to this knowledge they became one with Me. They need not come to birth even at a creation, nor do they suffer at a dissolution.

3. The great prakriti is for me the womb in which I deposit the germ; from it all beings come to birth.

4. Whatever forms take birth in the various species, the great prakriti is their Mother and I the seed-giving Father.

5. Sattva, rajas and tamas are the gunas sprung from prakriti; it is they, that keep the imperishable Dweller bound to the body.

* You must be the change you wish to see in the world.

6.   Of these sattva, being stainless, is light-giving and healing; it binds with the bond of happiness and the bond of knowledge.

7.   Rajas, know thou, is of the nature of passion, the source of thirst and attachment; it keeps man bound with the bond of action.

8.   Tamas, know thou, born of ignorance, is mortal man's delusion; it keeps him bound with heedlessness, sloth and slumber.

9.   Sattva attaches man to happiness, rajas to action, and tamas, shrouding knowledge, attaches him to heedlessness.

10.   Sattva prevails, having overcome rajas and tamas; rajas, when it has overpowered sattva and tamas; likewise tamas reigns when sattva and rajas are crushed.

11.   When the light—knowledge—shines forth from all the gates of this body, then it may be known that the sattva thrives.

12.   Greed, activity, assumption of undertakings, restlessness, craving—these are in evidence when rajas flourishes.

13.   Ignorance, dullness, heedlessness, and delusion—these are in evidence when tamas reigns.

14.   If the embodied one meets his end whilst sattva prevails, then he attains to the spotless worlds of the knowers of the Highest.

15.   If he dies during the reign within him of rajas, he is born among men attached to action; and if he dies in tamas, he is born in species not endowed with reason.

16.   The fruit of sattvika action is said to be stainless merit. That of rajas is pain and that of tamas ignorance.

17.   Those abiding in sattva rise upwards, those in rajas stay midway, those in tamas sink downwards.

18.   When the seer perceives no agent other than the gunas, and knows Him who is above the gunas, he attains to My being.

As soon as a man realizes that he is not the doer, but the gunas are the agent, the "self" vanishes, and he goes through all his actions spontaneously, just to sustain the body. And as the body is meant to subserve the highest end, all his actions will even reveal detachment and dispassion. Such a seer can easily have a glimpse of the One who is above the gunas and offer his devotion to Him.

19.　　When the embodied one transcends these three gunas which are born of his contact with the body, he is released from the pain of birth, death and age and attains deathlessness.

Arjuna Said:

20.　　What, O Lord, are the marks of him who has transcended the three gunas? How does he conduct himself? How does he transcend the three gunas?

The Lord Said:

21.　　He, who does not disdain light, activity, and delusion when they come into being, nor desires them when they vanish;

22.　　He, who seated as one indifferent, is not shaken by the gunas, and stays still and moves not, knowing it is gunas playing their parts;

23.　　He who holds pleasure and pain alike, who is sedate, who regards as same earth, stone and gold, who is wise and weighs in equal scale things pleasant and unpleasant, who is even-minded in praise and blame;

24.　　Who holds alike respect and disrespect, who is the same to friend and foe, who indulges in no undertakings—That man is called gunatita.

Shls. 22–25 must be read and considered together. Light activity and delusion, as we have seen in the foregoing shlokas, are the products or indications of sattva, rajas and tamas respectively. The inner meaning of these verses is that he who has transcended the gunas will be unaffected by them. A stone does not desire light, nor does it disdain activity or inertness; it is still, without having the will to be so. If someone puts it into motion, it does not fret; if again, it is allowed to lie still, it does not feel that inertness or delusion has seized it. The difference between a stone and a gunatita is that the latter has full consciousness and with full knowledge he shakes himself free from the bonds that bind an ordinary mortal. He has, as a result of his knowledge, achieved the purpose of a stone. Like the stone he is witness, but not the doer, of the activities of the gunas or prakriti. Of such jnani one may say that he is sitting still, unshaken in the knowledge that it is the gunas playing their parts. We who are every moment of our lives acting as though we are the doers can only imagine the state, we can hardly experience it. But we can hitch our wagon to that star and work our way closer and closer toward it by gradually withdrawing the self from our actions. A gunatita has experience of his own condition but he cannot describe it, for he who can describe it ceases to be one. The moment he proceeds to do so, "self" peeps in. The peace and light and bustle and inertness of our common experience are illusory. The Gita itself has made it clear in so many words that the sattvika state is the one nearest that of a gunatita. Therefore every one should strive to develop more and more sattva in himself, believing that some day he will reach the goal of the state of gunatita.

25. He who serves me in an unwavering and exclusive bhaktiyoga transcends these gunas and is worthy to become one with Brahman.

26. For I am the very image of Brahman, changeless and deathless, as also of everlasting dharma and perfect bliss.

Thus ends the fourteenth discourse, entitled "Gunatrayavibhaga Yoga" in the converse of Lord Krishna and Arjuna, on the science of Yoga, as part of the knowledge of Brahman, in the Upanishad called the Bhagawadgita.

Gandhi with his
supporters in the train

Discourse 15: The Supreme Person

This discourse deals with the supreme form of the Lord, transcending Kshara (perishable) and Akshara (imperishable).

The Lord Said:

1. With the root above and branches below, the ashvattha tree, they say, is impossible; it has Vedic hymns for its leaves; he who knows it knows the Vedas.

   Shvah means tomorrow, and ashvattha (nashvopi sthata) means that which will not last even until tomorrow, i.e., the world of sense which is every moment in a state of flux. But even though it is perpetually changing, as its root is Brahman or the Supreme, it is imperishable. It has for its protection and support the leaves of the Vedic hymns, i.e., dharma. He who knows the world of sense as such and who knows dharma is the real jnani, that man has really known the Vedas.

2. Above all and below its branches spread, blossoming because of the gunas, having for their shoots the sense-objects; deep down in the world of men are ramified its roots, in the shape of the consequences of action.

* *The weak can never forgive. Forgiveness is the attribute of the strong. (Gandhi at 10 Downing Street, London, office of the British Prime Minister)*

This is the description of the tree of the world of sense as the unenlightened see it. They fail to discover its Root above in Brahman and so they are always attached to the objects of sense. They water the tree with the three gunas and remain bound to Karman in the world of men.

3. Its form as such is not here perceived, neither is its end, nor beginning, nor basis. Let man first hew down this deep-rooted Ashvattha with the sure weapon of detachment;

4. Let him pray to win to that haven from which there is no return and seek to find refuge in the primal Being from whom has emanated this ancient world of action.

"Detachment" in shl. 3 here means dispassion, aversion to the objects of the senses. Unless man is determined to cut himself off from the temptations of the world of sense he will go deeper into the mire every day. These verses show that one dare not play with the objects of the senses with impunity.

5. To that imperishable haven those enlightened souls go—who are without pride and delusion, who have triumphed over the taints of attachment, who are ever in tune with the Supreme, whose passions have died, who are exempt from the pairs of opposites, such as pleasure and pain.

6. Neither the sun, nor the moon, nor fire illumine it; men who arrive there return not—that is My supreme abode.

7. As part indeed of Myself which has been the eternal Jiva in this world of life, attracts the mind and the five senses from their place in prakriti.

8. When the master (of the body) acquires a body and discards it he carries these with him wherever he goes, even as the wind carries scents from flower beds.

9. Having settled himself in the senses—ear, eye, touch, taste, and smell—as well as the mind, through them he frequents their objects.

These objects are the natural objects of the senses. The frequenting or enjoyment of these would be tainted if there were the sense of "I" about it; otherwise it is pure, even as a child's enjoyment of these objects is innocent.

10.   The deluded perceive Him not as He leaves or settles in (a body) or enjoys (sense objects) in association with the gunas; it is those endowed with the eye of knowledge who alone see Him.

11.   Yogins who strive see Him seated in themselves; the witless ones who have not cleansed themselves to see Him not, even though they strive.

This does not conflict with the covenant that God has made even with the sinner in discourse 9. Akritatman (who has not cleansed himself) means one who has no devotion in him, who has not made up his mind to purify himself. The most confirmed sinner, if he has humility enough to seek refuge in surrender to God, purifies himself and succeeds in finding Him. Those who do not care to observe the cardinal and the casual vows and expect to find God through bare intellectual exercise are witless, Godless; they will not find Him.

12.   The light in the sun which illumines the whole universe and which is in the moon and in fire that light, know thou, is Mine;

13.   It is I, who penetrating the earth uphold all beings with My strength, and becoming the moon—the essence of all sap— nourish all the herbs;

14.   It is I who becoming the Vaishvanara Fire and entering the bodies of all that breathe, assimilate the four kinds of food with the help of the outward and the inward breaths.

15.   And I am seated in the hearts of all, from Me proceed memory, knowledge and the dispelling of doubts; it is I who am to be known in all the Vedas, I, the author of Vedanta and the knower of the Vedas.

16.   There are two Beings in the world: kshara (perishable) and akshara (imperishable). Kshara embraces all creatures and their permanent basis is akshara.

17.   The Supreme Being is surely another—called Paramatman who is the Imperishable Ishvara pervades and supports the three worlds.

18.   Because I transcend the kshara and am also higher than the akshara, I am known in the world and in the Vedas as Purushottama (the Highest Being).

19.   He who, undeluded, knows Me as Purushottama, knows all, he worships Me with all his heart.

20.   Thus I have revealed to thee, sinless one, this most mysterious shastra; he who understands this is a man of understanding, he has fulfilled his life's mission.

Thus ends the fifteenth discourse, entitled "purushottama Yoga" in the converse of Lord Krishna and Arjuna, on the science of Yoga, as part of the knowledge of Brahman in the Upanishad called the Bhagawadgita.

Non-violence and peace are all best exemplified with one name – Mohandas Karamchand Gandhi (1869-1948), also known as Mahatma Gandhi. Residing in the minds of millions, Gandhiji was able to unite India like none other.

Discourse 16: The Godlike and the Demoniac

This discourse treats of the divine and the devilish heritage.

The Lord Said:

1. Fearlessness, purity of heart, steadfastness in jnana and yoga— knowledge and action, beneficence, self-restraint, sacrifice, spiritual study, austerity, and uprightness;

2. Non-violence, truth, slowness to wrath, the spirit of dedication, serenity, aversion to slander, tenderness to all that lives, freedom from greed, gentleness, modesty, freedom from levity;

3. Spiritedness, forgiveness, fortitude, purity, freedom from ill-will and arrogance—these are to be found in one born with the divine heritage.

4. Pretentiousness, arrogance, self-conceit, wrath, coarseness, ignorance—these are to be found in one born with the devilish heritage.

5. The divine heritage makes for Freedom, the devilish for bondage. Grieve not thou art born with a divine heritage.

6. There are two orders of created beings in this world—the divine and the devilish; the divine order has been described in detail, hear from Me now of the devilish.

* An eye for an eye makes the whole world blind.

7.   Men of the devil do not know what they may do and what they may not do; neither is there any purity, nor right conduct, nor truth to be found in them.

8.   "Without truth, without basis, without God is the universe," they say; "born of the union of the sexes, prompted by naught but lust."

9.   Holding this view, these depraved souls, of feeble understanding and of fierce deeds, come forth as enemies of the world to destroy it.

10.   Given to insatiable lust, possessed by pretentiousness, arrogance and conceit, they seize wicked purposes in their delusion, and go about pledged to uncleaned deeds.

11.   Given to boundless cares that end only with their death, making indulgence or lust their sole goal, convinced that that is all;

12.   Caught in a myriad snares of hope, slaves to lust and wrath, they speak unlawfully to amass wealth for the satisfaction of their appetites.

13.   "This have I gained today; this aspiration shall I now attain; this wealth is mine; this likewise shall be mine hereafter;"

14.   "This enemy I have already slain, others also I shall slay; lord of all am I; enjoyment is mine, perfection is mine, strength is mine, happiness is mine;"

15.   "Wealthy am I, and high-born. What other is like unto me? I shall perform a sacrifice! I shall give alms! I shall be merry!" Thus think they, by ignorance deluded;

16.   And tossed about by diverse fancies, caught in the net of delusion, stuck deep in the indulgence of appetites, into foul hell they fall.

17.   Wise in their own conceit, stubborn, full of the intoxication of
       pelf and pride, they offer nominal sacrifices for show, contrary
       to the rule.

18.   Given to pride, force, arrogance, lust and wrath they are
       deriders indeed, scorning Me in their own and other' bodies.

19.   These cruel scorners, lowest of mankind and vile, I hurl down
       again and again, into devilish wombs.

20.   Doomed to devilish wombs, these deluded ones, far from ever
       coming to Me, sink lower and lower in birth after birth.

21.   Three-fold is the gate of hell, leading man to perdition—Lust,
       Wrath, and Greed; these three, therefore, should be shunned.

22.   The man who escapes these three gates of Darkness works out
       his welfare and thence reaches the highest state.

23.   He who forsakes the rule of shastra and does but the bidding of
       his selfish desires, gains neither perfection, nor happiness, nor
       the highest state.

       *Shastra does not mean the rites and formulae laid down in the so-called
       dharmashastra, but the path of self-restraint laid down by the seers and
       the saints.*

24.   Therefore let shastra be thy authority for determining what
       ought to be done and what ought not to be done; ascertain
       thou the rule of the shastra and do thy task here (accordingly).

       *Shastra here too has the same meaning as in the preceding shloka. Let no
       one be a law unto himself, but take as his authority the law laid down by
       men who have known and lived religion.*

       *Thus ends the sixteenth discourse, entitled "Daivasurasampadvibhaga
       Yoga" in the converse of Lord Krishna and Arjuna, on the science of
       Yoga, as part of the knowledge of Brahman in the Upanishad called the
       Bhagawadgita.*

I have nothing new to teach the world.
Truth and Non-violence are as old as the
hills. All I have done is to try experiments
on both on as vast a scale as I could.

Discourse 17: The Three Kinds of Faith, Food, Sacrifices

On being asked to consider shastra (conduct of the worthy) as the authority, Arjuna is faced with a difficulty. What is the position of those who may not be able to accept the authority of Shastra but who may act in faith? An answer to the question is attempted in this discourse. Krishna rests content with pointing out the rocks and shoals on the path of the one who forsakes the beaconlight of Shastra (conduct of the worthy).

In doing so he deals with the faith and sacrifice, austerity and charity, performed with faith, and their divisions according to the spirit in which they are performed. He also sings the greatness of the mystic syllables AUM TAT SAT—a formula of dedication of all work to God.

Arjuna Said:

1. What, then is the position of those who forsake the rule of Shastra and yet worship with faith? Do they act from sattva or rajas or tamas?

The Lord Said:

2. Threefold is the faith of men, an expression of their nature in each case; it is sattvika, rajas or tamasa. Hear thou of it.

* No man loses his freedom except through his own weakness

3.   The faith of every man is in accord with his innate character; man is made up of faith; whatever his object of faith, even so is he.

4.   Sattvika persons worship the gods; rajas ones, the Yakshas and Rakshasas; and others—men of tamas—worship manes and spirits.

5.   Those men who, wedded to pretentiousness and arrogance, possessed by the violence of lust and passion, practice fierce austerity not ordained by shastra;

6.   They, whilst they torture the several elements that make up their bodies, torture Me too dwelling in them; know them to be of unholy resolves.

7.   Of three kinds again is the food that is dear to each; so also are sacrifice, austerity, and charity. Hear how they differ.

8.   Victuals that add to one's years, vitality, strength, health, happiness and appetite; are savory, rich, substantial and inviting, are dear to the sattvika.

9.   Victuals that are bitter, sour, salty, over-hot, spicy, dry, burning, and causing pain, bitterness and disease, are dear to rajasa.

10.   Food which has become cold, insipid, putrid, stale, discarded and unfit for sacrifice, is dear to the tamasa.

11.   That sacrifice is sattvika which is willingly offered as a duty without desire for fruit and according to the rule.

12.   But when sacrifice is offered with an eye to fruit and for vain glory, know, O Bharatashreshtha, that it is rajasa.

13.   Sacrifice which is contrary to the rule, which produces no food, which lacks the sacred text, which involves no giving up, which is devoid of faith is said to be tamasa.

14.   Homage to the gods, to Brahmanas, to gurus and to wise men; cleanliness, uprightness, brahmacharya and non-violence— these constitute austerity (tapas) of the body.

15.   Words that cause no hurt, that are true loving and helpful, and spiritual study constitute austerity of speech.

16.   Serenity, benignity, silence, self-restraint, and purity of the spirit—these constitute austerity of the mind.

17.   This threefold austerity practiced in perfect faith by men not desirous of fruit, and disciplined, is said to be sattvika.

18.   Austerity which is practiced with an eye to gain praise, honor and homage and for ostentation is said to be rajasa; it is fleeting and unstable.

19.   Austerity which is practiced from any foolish obsession, either to torture oneself or to procure another's ruin, is called tamasa.

20.   Charity, given as a matter of duty, without expectation of any return, at the right place and time, and to the right person is said to be sattvika.

21.   Charity, which is given either in hope of receiving in return, or with a view of winning merit, or grudgingly, is declared to be rajasa.

22.   Charity given at the wrong place and time, and to the undeserving recipient disrespectfully and with contempt is declared to be tamasa.

23.   AUM TAT SAT has been declared to be the threefold name of Brahman and by that name were created of old the Brahmanas, the Vedas and sacrifices.

24.   Therefore, with AUM ever on their lips, are all the rites of sacrifice, charity and austerity, performed always to the rule, by Brahmavadins.

25.   With the utterance of TAT and without the desire for fruit are the several rites of sacrifice, austerity and charity performed by those seeking Freedom.

26.   SAT is employed in the sense of "real" and "good;" SAT is also applied to beautiful deeds.

27.   Constancy in sacrifice, austerity and charity, is called SAT; and all work for those purposes is also SAT.

The substance of the last four shlokas is that every action should be done in a spirit of complete dedication to God. For AUM alone is the only Reality. That only which is dedicated to It counts.

28.   Whatever is done, O Partha, by way of sacrifice, charity or austerity or any other work, is called Asat if done without faith. It counts for naught hereafter as here.

Thus ends the seventeenth discourse, entitled "Sharaddhatrayavibhaga Yoga" in the converse of Lord Krishna and Arjuna, on the science of Yoga, as part of the knowledge of Brahman in the Upanishad called the Bhagawadgita.

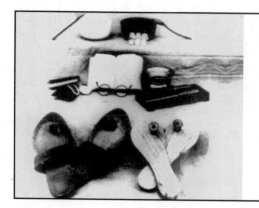

Gandhi's property at his death: his sandals, watch, bowl and plate, and round glasses.

Discourse 18: The Yoga of Release by Renunciation

This concluding discourse sums up the teaching of the Gita. It may be said to be summed up in the following: "Abandon all duties and come to Me, the only Refuge" (66). That is true renunciation.

But abandonment of all duties does not mean abandonment of actions; it means abandonment of the desire for fruit. Even the highest act of service must be dedicated to Him, without the desire. That is Tyaga (abandonment), that is Sannyasa (renunciation).

Arjuna Said:

1. I would fain learn severally the secret of sannyasa and of tyaga.

The Lord Said:

2. Renunciation of actions springing from selfish desire is known as sannyasa by the seers; abandonment of the fruit of all action is called tyaga by the wise.

3. Some thoughtful persons say: "All action should be abandoned as an evil;" others say: "Action for sacrifice, charity and austerity should not be relinquished."

4.   Hear my decision in this matter of tyaga, for tyaga, too has been described to be of three kinds.

5.   Action for sacrifice, charity and austerity may not be abandoned; it must needs be performed. Sacrifice, charity and austerity are purifiers of the wise.

6.   But even these actions should be performed abandoning all attachment and fruit; such, is my best and considered opinion.

7.   It is not right to renounce one's allotted task; its abandonment, from delusion, is said to be tamasa.

8.   He who abandons action, deeming it painful and for fear of straining his limbs, he will never gain the fruit of abandonment, for his abandonment is rajasa.

9.   But when an allotted task is performed from a sense of duty and with abandonment of attachment and fruit, that abandonment is deemed to be sattvika.

10.   Neither does he disdain unpleasant action, nor does he cling to pleasant action—this wise man full of sattva, who practices abandonment, and who has shaken off all doubts.

11.   For the embodied one cannot completely abandon action; but he who abandons the fruit of action is named a tyagi.

12.   To those who do not practice abandonment accrues, when they pass away, the fruit of action which is of three kinds: disagreeable, agreeable, mixed; but never to the sannyasins.

13.   Learn, from me, the five factors mentioned in the Sankhyan doctrine for the accomplishment of all action:

14.   The field, the doer, the various means, the several different operations, the fifth and the last, the Unseen.

15.   Whatever action, right or wrong, a man undertakes to do with the body, speech or mind, these are the five factors thereof.

16.   This being so, he who, by reason of unenlightened intellect, sees the unconditioned Atman as the agent—such a man is dense and unseeing.

17.   He who is free from all sense of "I," whose motive is untainted, slays not nor is bound, even though he slay all these worlds.

This shloka though seemingly somewhat baffling is not really so. The Gita on many occasions presents the ideal to attain which the aspirant has to strive but which may not be possible completely to realize in the world.

It is like definitions in geometry. A perfect straight line does not exist, but it is necessary to imagine it in order to prove the various propositions. Even so, it is necessary to hold up ideals of this nature as standards for imitation in matters of conduct. This then would seem to be the meaning of this shloka: He who has made ashes of "self," whose motive is untainted, may slay the whole world, if he will. But in reality he who has annihilated "self" has annihilated his flesh too, and he whose motive is untainted sees the past, present and future. Such a being can be one and only one— God. He acts and yet is no doer, slays and yet is no slayer. For mortal man and royal road—the conduct of the worthy—is ever before him, viz. ahimsa—holding all life sacred.

18.   Knowledge, the object of knowledge, and the knower compose the threefold urge to action; the means, the action and the doer compose the threefold sum of action.

19.   Knowledge, action, and the doer are of three kinds according to their different gunas; hear thou these, just as they have been described in the science of the gunas.

20.   Know that knowledge whereby one sees in all beings immutable entity—a unity in diversity—to be sattvika.

21. That knowledge which perceives separately in all beings several entities of diverse kinds, know thou to be rajasa.

22. And knowledge which, without reason, clings to one single thing, as though it were everything, which misses the true essence and is superficial is tamasa.

23. That action is called sattvika which, being one's allotted task, is performed without attachment, without like or dislike, and without a desire for fruit.

24. That action which is prompted by the desire for fruit, or by the thought of "I," and which involves much dissipation of energy is called rajasa.

25. That action which is blindly undertaken without any regard to capacity and consequences, involving loss and hurt, is called tamasa.

26. That doer is called sattvika who has shed all attachment, all thought of "I," who is filled with firmness and zeal, and who seeks neither success nor failure.

27. That doer is said to be rajasa who is passionate, desirous of the fruit of action, greedy, violent, unclean, and moved by joy and sorrow.

28. That doer is called tamasa who is undisciplined, vulgar, stubborn, knavish, spiteful, indolent, woebegone, and dilatory.

29. Hear now, detailed fully and severally, the threefold division of understanding and will, according to their gunas.

30. That understanding is sattvika which knows action from inaction, what ought to be done from what ought not to be done, fear from fearlessness and bondage from release.

31. That understanding is rajasa, which decides erroneously between right and wrong, between what ought to be done and what ought not to be done.

32.   That understanding is tamasa, which, shrouded in darkness, thinks wrong to be right and mistakes everything for its reverse.

33.   That will is sattvika which maintains an unbroken harmony between the activities of the mind, the vital energies and the senses.

34.   That will is rajasa which clings, with attachment, to righteousness, desire and wealth, desirous of fruit in each case.

35.   That will is tamasa, whereby insensate man does not abandon sleep, fear, grief, despair and self-conceit.

36.   Hear now from Me the three kinds of pleasure. Pleasure which is enjoyed only by repeated practice, and which puts an end to pain.

37.   Which, in its inception, is as poison, but in the end as nectar, born of the serene realization of the true nature of Atman— that pleasure is said to be sattvika.

38.   That pleasure is called rajasa which, arising from the contact of the senses with their objects, is at first as nectar but in the end like poison.

39.   That pleasure is called tamasa which arising from sleep and sloth and heedlessness, stupefies the soul both at first and in the end.

40.   There is no being, either on earth or in heaven among the gods, that can be free from these three gunas born of prakriti.

41.   The duties of Brahmanas, Kshatriyas, Vaishyas, and Shudras, are distributed according to their innate qualifications.

42.   Serenity, self-restraint, austerity, purity, forgiveness, uprightness, knowledge and discriminative knowledge, faith in God are the Brahmana's natural duties.

43.   Valor, spiritedness, constancy, resourcefulness, not fleeing from battle, generosity, and the capacity to rule are the natural duties of a Kshatriya.

44.   Tilling the soil, protection of the cow and commerce are the natural functions of a Vaishya, while service is the natural duty of a Shudra.

45.   Each man, by complete absorption in the performance of his duty, wins perfection. Hear now how he wins such perfection by devotion to that duty.

46.   By offering the worship of his duty to Him who is the moving spirit of all beings, and by whom all this is pervaded, man wins perfection.

47.   Better one's own duty, though uninviting, than another's which may be more easily performed; doing duty which accords with one's nature, one incurs no sin.

The central teaching of the Gita is detachment — abandonment of the fruit of action. And there would be no room for this abandonment if one were to prefer another's duty to one's own. Therefore one's own duty is said to be better than another's. It is the spirit in which duty is done that matters, and its unattached performance is its own reward.

48.   One should not abandon, that duty to which one is born, imperfect though it be; for all action, in its inception, is enveloped in imperfection, as fire in smoke.

49.   He who has weaned himself of all kinds, who is master of himself, who is dead to desire, attains through renunciation the perfection of freedom from action.

50.   Learn now from Me, in brief how he who has gained this perfection, attains to Brahman, the supreme consummation of knowledge.

51.   Equipped with purified understanding, restraining the self with firm will, abandoning sound and other objects of the senses, putting aside likes and dislikes,

52. Living in solitude, spare in diet, restrained in speech, body and mind, ever absorbed in dhyanayoga, anchored in dispassion.

53. Without pride, violence, arrogance, lust, wrath, possession, having shed all sense of "mine" and at peace with himself, he is fit to become one with Brahman.

54. One with Brahman and at peace with himself, he grieves not, nor desires; holding all beings alike, he achieves supreme devotion to Me.

55. By devotion, he realizes in truth how great I am, who I am; and having known Me in reality he enters into Me.

56. Even whilst always performing actions, he who makes Me his refuge wins, by My grace, the eternal and imperishable haven.

57. Casting, with thy mind, all actions on Me, make Me thy goal, and resorting to the yoga of even-mindedness fix thy thought ever on Me.

58. Fixing his thy thought on Me, thou shalt surmount all obstacles by My grace; but if possessed by the sense of "I" thou listen not, thou shalt perish.

59. If obsessed by the sense of "I," thou thinkest, "I will not fight," vain is thy obsession; (thy) nature will compel thee.

60. What thou wilt not do because of thy delusion, thou shalt do, even against thy will, bound as thou art by the duty to which thou art born.

61. God dwells in the heart of every being and by His delusive mystery whirls them all, (as though) set on a machine.

62. In Him alone seek thy refuge with all thy heart. By His grace shalt thou win to the eternal haven of supreme peace.

63. Thus have I expounded to thee the most mysterious of all knowledge; ponder over it fully, then act as thou wilt.

64.   Hear again My supreme word, the most mysterious of all; dearly beloved thou art of Me, hence I desire to declare thy welfare.

65.   On Me fix thy mind, to Me bring thy devotion, to Me offer thy sacrifice, to Me make thy obeisance; to Me indeed shalt thou come—solemn is My promise to thee, thou art dear to Me.

66.   Abandon all duties and come to Me the only refuge. I will release thee from all sins; grieve not!

67.   Utter this never to him who knows no austerity, has no devotion, nor any desire to listen, nor yet to him who scoffs at Me.

68.   He who will propound this supreme mystery to My devotees, shall, by that act of highest devotion to Me, surely come to Me.

69.   Nor among men is there any who renders dearer service to Me than he; nor shall there be on earth any more beloved by Me than he. It is only he who has himself gained the knowledge and lived it in his life that can declare it to others. These two shlokas cannot possibly have any reference to him, who no matter how he conducts himself, can give flawless reading and interpretation of the Gita.

70.   And the man of faith who, scorning not, will but listen to it—even he shall be released and will go to the happy worlds of men of virtuous deeds.

72.   Hast thou heard this with a concentrated mind? Has thy delusion, born of ignorance, been destroyed?

Arjuna Said:

73.   Thanks to Thy grace, my delusion is destroyed, my understanding has returned. I stand secure, my doubts all dispelled; I will do thy bidding.

Sanjaya Said:

74. Thus did I hear this marvelous and thrilling discourse between Vasudeva and the great-souled Partha.

75. It was by Vyasa's favor that I listened to this supreme and mysterious Yoga as expounded by the lips of the Master of Yoga, Krishna Himself.

76. O King, as often as I recall that marvelous and purifying discourse between Keshava and Arjuna, I am filled with recurring rapture.

77. And as often as I recall that marvelous form of Hari, my wonder knows no bounds and I rejoice again and again.

78. Wheresoever Krishna, the Master of Yoga, is, and wheresoever is Partha the Bowman, there rest assured are Fortune, Victory, Prosperity, and Eternal Right.

Thus ends the eighteenth discourse, entitled "Sannyasa Yoga" in the converse of Lord Krishna and Arjuna, on the science of Yoga, as part of the knowledge of Brahman in the Upanishad called the Bhagawadgita.

PART 3

Gandhi Comments on Bhagavad-Gita

The Gita is the Universal mother. She turns away nobody. Her door is wide open to anyone who knocks. A true votary of Gita does not know what disappointment is. He ever dwells in perennial joy and peace that passeth understanding. But that peace and joy come not to skeptic or to him who is proud of his intellect or learning.

It is reserved only for the humble in spirit who brings to her worship a fullness of faith and an undivided singleness of mind. There never was a man who worshipped her in that spirit and went disappointed. I find a solace in the Bhagavad Gita that I miss even in the Sermon on the Mount.

When disappointment stares me in the face and all alone I see not one ray of light, I go back to the Bhagavad Gita. I find a verse here and a verse there, and I immediately begin to smile in the midst of overwhelming tragedies – and my life has been full of external tragedies- and if they have left no visible or indelible scar on me, I owe it all to the teaching of the Bhagavad Gita.

INFLUENCES OF THE BHAGAVAD GITA

on Mahatma Gandhi

- Gandhi was sufficiently impressed and in accordance with the advice of these brothers (Gandhi was studying Law in England), read the English translation of this poem by Sir Edwin Arnold and was captivated for life by the message of the Gita.

- Lord Krishna is the personification of wisdom in the opinion of Gandhi The Bhagvad Gita advocates the path of Karma or selfless action and its message is the renunciation of the fruit of action

- When disappointment stares me in the face and when I am all alone and I do not see even one ray of light , I go back to the Bhagvad Gita

- During his imprisonment, he made a detailed study of this epic poem and on his friends insistence translated the Gita into Gujarati.

Reference (Online):

1. http://blog.meditation-presence.com/compassion/gandhi-and-the-bhagavad-gita/

2. http://www.michellemyhre.com/2011/04/gandhi-on-bhagavad-gita.html#!/2011/04/gandhi-   on-bhagavad-gita.html

NAMASTE
THE UNIVERSAL GREETING

Namaste is a complete sentence made up of two words, *Namas* and *Te*. It means "I honor the place in you in which the entire universe dwells, the place in you which is of truth, of light and of peace. However, "You" refers not to the physical person but the inner being. Thus the deeper meaning is "the divinity in me greets the divinity in you." This greeting transcends race, religion or nationality, can be used day or night, in all circumstances, in any place, to stranger or friend of any gender, age, or social status.

Namaste is also the most hygienic way of conveying respect, Discipline, and culture. Because the parties do not physically contact each other there is no fear of passing on infections like flu as you may in shaking hands, hugging or kissing. The words are usually accompanied by a *slight bow* made with hands pressed together, palms touching and fingers pointed upward, in front of the chest. In so doing you share a sense of grace, humility and peace. It was used in India for thousands of years and is now universally recognized as the most dignified means by which two souls can demonstrate mutual respect and love.

It was a distinctive characteristic of Mahatma Gandhi who made humility and simple truth more powerful than empires.

www.dharmaeducation.info.

APPENDIX I

GANDHI'S VIEWS ON CONVERSION

GANDHI'S VIEW ON MISSIONARIES

I believe that there is no such thing as conversion from one faith to another in the accepted sense of the word. It is a highly personal matter for the individual and his God. I may not have any design upon my neighbor as to his faith which I must honor even as I honor my own. Having reverently studied the scriptures of the world I could no more think of asking a Christian or a Musalman, or a Parsi or a Jew to change his faith than I would think of changing my own. (Harijan, September 9,1935)

I DISBELIEVE IN CONVERSION

I disbelieve in the conversion of one person by another. My effort should never to be to undermine another's faith. This implies true humility. (*Young India*, April 23, 1931)

CONVERSION: IMPEDIMENT TO PEACE

It is impossible for me to reconcile myself to the idea of conversion after the style that goes on in India and elsewhere today. It is an error which is perhaps the greatest impediment to the world's progress toward peace...Why should a Christian want to convert a Hindu to Christianity ? Why should he not be satisfied if the Hindu is a good or godly man? (*Harijan*, January 30,1937)

NO CONVERSION DESIGNS UPON ME

I am not interested in weaning you from Christianity and making you Hindu, and I do not relish your designs upon me, if you had any, to convert me to Christianity. I would also dispute your claim that Christianity is the only true religion (*Harijan*, June 3, 1937)

CONVERSION

Conversion must not mean denationalization. Conversion should mean a definite giving up of the evil of the old. adoption of all the good of the new and a scrupulous avoidance of everything evil in the new. Conversion, therefore, should mean a life of greater dedication to one's country, greater surrender to God, greater self-purification. (*Young India*, August 20, 1925)

APING OF EUROPEANS AND AMERICANS

As I wander about through the length and breadth of India I see many Christian Indians almost ashamed of their birth, certainly of their ancestral religion, and of their ancestral dress. The aping of Europeans by Anglo-Indians is bad enough, but the aping of them by Indian converts is a violence done to their country and, shall I say, even to their new religion. (*Young India*, August 8, 1925)

WHY SHOULD I CHANGE MY RELIGION ?

I hold that proselytisation under the cloak of humanitarian work is unhealthy to say the least. It is most resented by people here. Religion after all is a deep personal thing. It touches the heart. Why I should change my religion because the doctor who professes Christianity as his religion has cured me of some disease, or why should the doctor expect me to change whilst I am under his influence ? (*Young India*, April 23, 1931)

MISSIONARY AIM: UPROOTING HINDUISM

My fear is that though Christian friends nowadays do not say or admit it that Hindu religion is untrue, they must harbor in their breast that Hinduism is an error and that Christianity, as they believe it, is the only true religion...so far as one can understand the present (Christian) effort, it is to uproot Hinduism from her very foundation and replace it by another faith (*Harijan*, March 13, 1937)

WHY I AM NOT A CONVERT ?

Hinduism as I know it entirely satisfies my soul, fills my whole being...
When doubts haunt me, when disappointments stare me in the face, and
when I see not one ray of light on the horizon, I turn to the Bhagavad Gita,
and find a verse to comfort me; and I immediately begin to smile in the
midst of overwhelming sorrow. My life has been full of tragedies and if
they have not left any visible and indelible effect on me, I owe it to the
teachings of the Bhagavad Gita. (*Young India*, June 8, 1925)

UNDERMINING PEOPLE'S FAITH

The first distinction I would like to make...between your missionary work
and mine is that while I am strengthening the faith of people, you
(missionaries) are undermining it. (*Young India*, November 8, 1927)

PHYSICIAN HEAL YOURSELF

Conversion nowadays has become a matter of business, like any other
...India (Hindus) is in no need of conversion of this kind... Conversion in
the sense of self-purification, self-realization, is the crying need of the
times. That however is never what is meant by proselytisation. To those
who would convert India (Hindus), might it not be said, "Physician, heal
yourself." (*Young India*, April 23, 1931)

MISSIONARIES: VENDORS OF GOODS

When the missionary of another religion goes to them, he goes like a
vendor of goods. He has no special spiritual merit that will distinguish
him from those to whom he goes. He does however possess material goods
which he promises to those who will come to his fold. (Harijan, April 3,
1931)

IF I HAD THE POWER AND COULD I LEGISLATE...

If I had the power and could legislate, I should stop all proselytizing ...In
Hindu households the advent of a missionary has meant the disruption
of the family coming in the wake of change of dress, manners, language,
food and drink...(November 5, 1935)

THE ONLY BEGOTTEN SON OF GOD ?

I regard Jesus as a great teacher of humanity, but I do not regard him as the only begotten son of God. That epithet in its material interpretation is quite unacceptable. Metaphorically we are all sons of God, but for each of us there may be different sons of God in a special sense. Thus for me Chaitanya may be the only begotten son of God...God cannot be the exclusive divinity to Jesus. (*Harijan*, June 3, 1937)

WESTERN CHRISTIANITY TODAY

It is my firm opinion that Europe (and the United States) does not represent the spirit of God or Christianity...and Satan's successes are the greatest when appears with the name of God on his lips. (*Young India*, September 8, 1920)

WESTERN CHRISTIANITY

I consider western Christianity in its practical working a negation of Christ's Christianity. I cannot conceive Jesus, if he was living in flesh in our midst, approving of modern Christian organizations, public worship, or ministry.

APPENDIX II

In Praise of Bhagavad Gita

Great Comments by Great People
(Reference: Google Search Engine)

1. For thousands of years, the Bhagavad Gita has inspired millions of readers. Here's what some of the greats have to say in praise of this venerable scripture.

    "When I read the Bhagavad-Gita and reflect about how God created this universe everything else seems so superfluous." ~ **Albert Einstein**

    "The Bhagavad-Gita has a profound influence on the spirit of mankind by its devotion to God which is manifested by actions." ~ **Dr. Albert Schweizer**

2. "The Bhagavad-Gita is the most systematic statement of spiritual evolution of endowing value to mankind. It is one of the most clear and comprehensive summaries of perennial philosophy ever revealed; hence its enduring value is subject not only to India but to all of humanity." ~ **Aldous Huxley**

3. "The Bhagavad-Gita is a true scripture of the human race a living creation rather than a book, with a new message for every age and a new meaning for every civilization." ~ **Rishi Aurobindo**

4. "The idea that man is like unto an inverted tree seems to have been current in by gone ages. The link with Vedic conceptions is provided by Plato in his Timaeus in which it states..." behold we are not an earthly but a heavenly plant." ~ **Carl Jung**

5. "In the morning I bathe my intellect in the stupendous and cosmogonal philosophy of the Bhagavad-Gita, in comparison with which our modern world and its literature seems puny and trivial." ~ **Henry David Thoreau**

6. "The marvel of the Bhagavad-Gita is its truly beautiful revelation of life's wisdom which enables philosophy to blossom into religion." ~ **Herman Hesse**

7. "The Bhagavad-Gita calls on humanity to dedicate body, mind and soul to pure duty and not to become mental voluptuaries at the mercy of random desires and undisciplined impulses."

    "When doubts haunt me, when disappointments stare me in the face, and I see not one ray of hope on the horizon, I turn to Bhagavad-Gita and find a verse to comfort me; and I immediately begin to smile in the midst of overwhelming sorrow. Those who meditate on the Gita will derive fresh joy and new meanings from it every day."~ **Mahatma Gandhi**

8. "The Bhagavad-Gita deals essentially with the spiritual foundation of human existence. It is a call of action to meet the obligations and duties of life; yet keeping in view the spiritual nature and grander purpose of the universe." ~ **Pandit Jawaharlal Nehru**

9. "I owed a magnificent day to the Bhagavad-Gita. It was the first of books; it was as if an empire spoke to us, nothing small or unworthy, but large, serene, consistent, the voice of an old intelligence which in another age and climate had pondered and thus disposed of the same questions which exercise us."

    "The Bhagavad-Gita is an empire of thought and in its philosophical teachings Krishna has all the attributes of the full-fledged monotheistic deity and at the same time the attributes of the Upanisadic absolute." ~Ralph Waldo Emerson

10. "In order to approach a creation as sublime as the Bhagavad-Gita with full understanding it is necessary to attune our soul to it." ~ **Rudolph Steiner**

11. "From a clear knowledge of the Bhagavad-Gita all the goals of human existence become fulfilled. Bhagavad-Gita is the manifest quintessence of all the teachings of the Vedic scriptures." ~ **Adi Sankara**

12. "The Bhagavad-Gita is not separate from the Vaisnava philosophy and the Srimad Bhagavatam fully reveals the true import of this doctrine which is transmigration of the soul. On perusal of the first

chapter of Bhagavad-Gita one may think that they are advised to engage in warfare. When the second chapter has been read it can be clearly understood that knowledge and the soul is the ultimate goal to be attained. On studying the third chapter it is apparent that acts of righteousness are also of high priority. If we continue and patiently take the time to complete the Bhagavad-Gita and try to ascertain the truth of its closing chapter we can see that the ultimate conclusion is to relinquish all the conceptualized ideas of religion which we possess and fully surrender directly unto the Supreme Lord." ~ **Swami Prabhupada**

13. "The secret of karma yoga which is to perform actions without any fruitive desires is taught by Lord Krishna in the Bhagavad-Gita."

    "It is a bouquet composed of the beautiful flowers of spiritual truths, collected from the Vedas and the Upanishads."~ **Vivekananda**

14. No work in all Indian literature is more quoted, because none is better loved, in the West, than the Bhagavad-Gita. Translation of such a work demands not only knowledge of Sanskrit, but an inward sympathy with the theme and a verbal artistry. For the poem is a symphony in which God is seen in all things. . . . The Swami does a real service for students by investing the beloved Indian epic with fresh meaning. Whatever our outlook may be, we should all be grateful for the labor that has lead to this illuminating work."~**Dr. Geddes MacGregor**, Emeritus Distinguished Professor of Philosophy University of Southern California

15. The Gita can be seen as the main literary support for the great religious civilization of India, the oldest surviving culture in the world. The present translation and commentary is another manifestation of the permanent living importance of the Gita. ~**Thomas Merton**, Theologian

16. I am most impressed with A.C . Bhaktivedanta Swami Prabhupada's scholarly and authoritative edition of Bhagavad-Gita. It is a most valuable work for the scholar as well as the layman and is of great utility as a reference book as well as a textbook. I promptly recommend this edition to my students. It is a beautifully done book. ~**Dr. Samuel D. Atkins** Professor of Sanskrit, Princeton University

17. If truth is what works, as Pierce and the pragmatists insist, there must be a kind of truth in the Bhagavad-Gita As It Is, since those who follow its teachings display a joyous serenity usually missing in the bleak and strident lives of contemporary people.
~**Dr. Elwin H. Powell** Professor of Sociology State University of New York, Buffalo

18. It is a deeply felt, powerfully conceived and beautifully explained work. I don't know whether to praise more this translation of the Bhagavad-gita, its daring method of explanation, or the endless fertility of its ideas. I have never seen any other work on the Gita with such an important voice and style. . . . It will occupy a significant place in the intellectual and ethical life of modern man for a long time to come." ~**Dr. Shaligram Shukla** Professor of Linguistics, Georgetown University

19. The Bhagavad-Gita is not separate from the Vaishnava philosophy and the Srimad Bhagavatam fully reveals the true import of this doctrine which is transmigration of the soul. On perusal of the first chapter of Bhagavad-Gita one may think that they are advised to engage in warfare. When the second chapter has been read it can be clearly understood that knowledge and the soul is the ultimate goal to be attained. On studying the third chapter it is apparent that acts of righteousness are also of high priority. If we continue and patiently take the time to complete the Bhagavad-Gita and try to ascertain the truth of its closing chapter we can see that the ultimate conclusion is to relinquish all the conceptualized ideas of religion which we possess and fully surrender directly unto the Supreme Lord. ~**Bhaktisiddhanta Saraswati**

20. **I believe that in all the living languages of the world, there is no book so full of true knowledge, and yet so handy. It teaches self-control, austerity, non-violence, compassion, obedience to the call of duty for the sake of duty, and putting up a fight against unrighteousness (Adharma). To my knowledge, there is no book in the whole range of the world's literature so high above as the Bhagavad-Gita, which is the treasure-house of Dharma nor only for the Hindus but foe all mankind. ~M. M. Malaviya**

Reference (Online):

1. http://hinduism.about.com/od/thegita/a/famousquotes.htm
2. http://www.bhagavad-gita.us/articles/662/1/Famous-Reflections-on-the-Bhagavad-Gita/Page 1.html
3. http://newbhagavadgita.blogspot.com/2009/01/praise-for-new-bhagavad-gita.html
4. http://www.prabhupadanugas.eu/?p=2211
5. http://surrealist.org/people/bhagavad-gita1.html
6. http://www.asitis.com/reviews/

APPENDIX III

QUOTES FROM THE BHAGAVAD GITA

The Wisdom of the Bhagavad Gita

1. Better indeed is knowledge than mechanical practice. Better than knowledge is meditation. But better still is surrender of attachment to results, because there follows immediate peace.

2. Neither in this world nor elsewhere is there any happiness in store for him who always doubts.

3. Delusion arises from anger. The mind is bewildered by delusion. Reasoning is destroyed when the mind is bewildered. One falls down when reasoning is destroyed.

4. Man is made by his belief. As he believes, so he is.

5. The mind is restless and difficult to restrain, but it is subdued by practice.

6. There has never been a time when you and I have not existed, nor there a time when we will cease to exist. As the same person inhabits the body through childhood, youth, and old age, so too at the time of death he attains another body. The wise are not deluded by these changes.

7. Those that eat too much or eat too little, who sleep too much or sleep too little, will not succeed in meditation. But those who are temperate in eating and sleeping, work and recreation, will come to the end of sorrow through meditation.

8. Still your mind in me, still yourself in me, and without a doubt you shall be united with me, Lord of Love, dwelling in your heart.

9. The soul who meditates on the Self is content to serve the Self and rests satisfied within the Self; there remains nothing more for him to accomplish.

10. Fear Not. What is not real, never was and never will be. What is real, always was and cannot be destroyed.

11. Not by refraining from action does man attain freedom from action. Not by mere renunciation does he attain supreme perfection.

12. Action is greater than inaction. Perform therefore thy task in life. Even the life of the body could not be if there were no action.

13. When the sage climbs the heights of Yoga, he follows the path of work; but when he reaches the heights of Yoga, he is in the land of peace.

14. Whenever the mind unsteady and restless strays away from the spirit, let him ever and forever lead it again to the spirit.

15. No work stains a man who is pure, who is in harmony, who is master of his life, whose soul is one with the soul of all.

16. Make your mind one-pointed in meditation, and your heart will be purified. . . . With all fears dissolved in the peace of the Self and all desires dedicated to Brahman, controlling the mind and fixing it on me (God), sit in meditation with me as your only goal. With senses and mind constantly controlled through meditation, united with the Self within, an aspirant attains nirvana, the state of abiding joy and peace in me.

Reference (Online)

1. www.SuccessConsciousness.com
2. http://www.finestquotes.com/author_quotes-author-Bhagavad%20Gita-page-0.htm
3. http://www.mysticsaint.info/2006/06/wisdom-from-bhagavad-gita.html

APPENDIX IV

Swami Vivekananda's Speeches

(Swami Vivekananda attended the World Parliament of Religions at Chicago from 11th September 1893 to 27th September 1893. He represented Hindu Religion and spoke on six occasions: 11th, 15th, 19th, 26th, and 27th September. His speeches require to be studied in more depth, for they are the forerunners of the Universal Religion to come.)

Excerpt: (http://www.oocities.org/neovedanta/a32a.html)

Just five words "Sisters and Brothers of America" and the whole audience of seven thousand people rose to their feet and continued clapping for full three minutes; is this not a wonder? The speaker had never spoken on public platform; he had not come prepared with any written or pre-planned speech; he was just thirty years of age; still he captured the attention and adoration of foreign, learned, wealthy, and intelligent audience. Mother Saraswati, Goddess of Learning, put spiritual power in every word he spoke. And no wonder, that power reached the hearts of all, not only to those who were in the hall, but also to the hearts of those who were outside that building. It reached the persons in media and newspaper offices; it reached the learned professors and scholars, and it enlightened the ordinary and the special. The heart of America, as if, was affected by the spiritual fervour of the Swami.

What was so special about Swami Vivekananda's speech and words? The Swami was, first and foremost, a man of the Spirit, who had realized the ultimate Truth at the Holy feet of his Master. This was the most prominent facet of his multisided personality. His addresses were the manifestations of "Divinity within". Every word fist touched the Spirit, and then reached the ears of the listeners. The words were pregnant with truth, Eternal Truth. Those words had no limitations of time and place; those were not his, they represented the Truth of the past, present, and future. It was the perennial message of Vedanta, ever fresh and unchangeable. Those words defined the Truth: the Reality that never changes.

WELCOME ADDRESS - The World Parliament of Religions, Chicago
(http://www.theuniversalwisdom.org/hinduism/paper-on-hinduism-vivekananda/#more-5)

Response to Welcome At The World's Parliament of Religions
Chicago, 11th September 1893

Sisters and Brothers of America, It fills my heart with joy unspeakable to rise in response to the warm and cordial welcome which you have given us. I thank you in the name of the most ancient order of monks in the world; I thank you in the name of the mother of religions; and I thank you in the name of the millions and millions of Hindu people of all classes and sects. My thanks, also, to some of the speakers on this platform who, referring to the delegates from the Orient, have told you that these men from far-off nations may well claim the honor of bearing to different lands the idea of toleration. I am proud to belong to a religion which has taught the world both tolerance and universal acceptance. We believe not only in universal toleration, but we accept all religions as true. I am proud to belong to a nation which has sheltered the persecuted and the refugees of all religions and all nations of the earth. I am proud to tell you that we have gathered in our bosom the purest remnant of the Israelites, who came to the southern India and took refuge with us in the very year in which their holy temple was shattered to pieces by Roman tyranny. I am proud to belong to the religion which has sheltered and is still fostering the remnant of the grand Zoroastrian nation. I will quote to you, brethren, a few lines from a hymn which I remember to have repeated from my earliest boyhood, which is every day repeated by millions of human beings:

As the different streams having there sources in different places all mingle their water in the sea, so, O Lord, the different paths which men take through different tendencies, various though they appear, crooked or straight, all lead to Thee.

The present convention, which is one of the most august assemblies ever held, is in itself a vindication, a declaration to the world, of the wonderful doctrine preached in the Gita:

Whosoever comes to Me, through whatsoever form, I reach him; all men are struggling through paths which in the end lead to Me.

Sectarianism, bigotry, and it's horrible descendant, fanaticism, have long possessed this beautiful earth. They have filled the earth with violence, drenched it often and often with human blood, destroyed civilization, and sent whole nations to despair. Had it not been for these horrible demons, human society would be far more advanced than it is now. But their time is come; and I fervently hope that the bell that tolled this morning in honor of this convention may be the death-knell of all fanaticism, of all persecutions with the sword or with the pen, and of all uncharitable feelings between persons wending their way to the same goal.

Why we disagree? by Swami Vivekananda
Speech At The World's Parliament of Religions
Chicago, 15th September 1893

I will tell you a little story. You have heard the eloquent speaker who has just finished say, "Let us cease from abusing each other," and he was very sorry that there should be always so much variance.

But I think I should tell you a story which would illustrate the cause of this variance. A frog lived in a well. It had lived there for a long time. It was born there and brought up there, and yet was a little, small frog. Of course, the evolutionists were not there then to tell us whether the frog lost its eyes or not, but, for our story's sake, we must take it for granted that it had its eyes, and that it every day cleansed the water of all the worms and bacilli that lived in it with an energy that would do credit to our modern bacteriologists. In this way it went on and became a little sleek and fat. Well, one day another flog that lived in the sea came and fell into the well.

"Where are you from?"

"I am from the sea."

"The sea! How big is that? Is it as big as my well?" and he took a leap from one side of the well to the other.

"My friend," said the frog of the sea, "how do you compare the sea with your little well?"

Then the frog took another leap and asked, "Is your sea so big?"

"What nonsense you speak, to compare the sea with your well!"

"Well, then," said the frog of the well, "nothing can be bigger than my well; there can be nothing bigger than this; this fellow is a liar, so turn him out."

That has been the difficulty all the while.

I am a Hindu. I am sitting in my own little well and thinking that the whole world is my little well. The Christian sits in his little well and thinks the whole world is his well. The Mohammedan sits in his little well and thinks that is the whole world. I have to thank you of America for the great attempt you are making to break down the barriers of this little world of ours, and hope that, in the future, the Lord will help you to accomplish your purpose.

PAPER ON HINDUISM

Vivekananda at World Parliament of Religion:
Chicago, 19th September 1893

Three religions now stand in the world which have come down to us from time prehistoric - Hinduism, Zoroastrianism, and Judaism. They have all received tremendous shocks, and all of them prove by their survival their internal strength. But while Judaism failed to absorb Christianity and was driven out of its place of birth by its all-conquering daughter, and a handful of Parsees is all that remains to tell the tale of their grand religion, sect after sect arose in India and seemed to shake the religion of the Vedas to its very foundations, but like the waters of the sea-shore in a tremendous earthquake it receded only for a while, only to return in an all-absorbing flood, a thousand times more vigorous, and when the tumult of the rush was over, these sects were all sucked in, absorbed and assimilated into the immense body of the mother faith. From the high spiritual flights of the Vedanta philosophy, of which the latest discoveries of science seem like echoes, to the low ideas of idolatry with its multifarious mythology, the agnosticism of the Buddhists and the atheism of the Jains, each and all have a place in the Hindu's religion.

Where then, the question arises, where is the common center to which all these widely diverging radii converge? Where is the common basis upon which all these seemingly hopeless contradictions rest? And this is the question I shall at- tempt to answer.

The Hindus have received their religion through revelation, the Vedas. They hold that the Vedas are without beginning and without end. It may sound ludicrous to this audience, how a book can be without beginning or end. But by the Vedas no books are meant. They mean the accumulated treasury of spiritual laws discovered by different persons in different times. Just as the law of gravitation existed before its discovery, and would exist if all humanity forgot it, so is it with the laws that govern the spiritual relations between soul and soul and between individual spirits and the Father of all spirits were there before their discovery, and would remain even if we forgot them.

The discoverers of these laws are called Rishis, and we honor them as perfected beings. I am glad to tell this audience that some of the very greatest of them were women.

Here it may be said that these laws as laws may be without end, but they must have had a beginning. The Vedas teach us that creation is without beginning or end. Science is said to have proved that the sum total of cosmic energy is always the same. Then, if there was a time when nothing existed, where was all this manifested energy? Some say it was in a potential form in God. In that case God is sometimes potential and sometimes kinetic, which would make Him mutable? Everything mutable is a compound and everything compound must undergo that change which is called destruction. So God would die, which is absurd-Therefore, there never was a time when there was no creation.

If I may be allowed to use a simile, creation and creator are two lines, without beginning and without end, zoning parallel to each other. God is the ever-active providence, by whose power systems after systems are being evolved out of chaos, made to run for a time, and again destroyed. This is what the Brahmin boy repeats every day:

'The sun and the moon, the Lord created like the suns and the moons of previous cycles.'

And this agrees with modern science. Here I Stand and if I shut my eyes, and try to conceive my existence, 'I,' 'I,' 'I', what is the idea before me? The idea of a body. Am I, then, nothing but a combination of material substances? The Vedas declare, 'No' I am a spirit living in a body: I am not the body. The body will die, but I shall not die. Here I am in this body; it will fall, bull shall go on living. I had also a past. The soul was not created, for creation means a combination, which means a certain future dissolution. If then the soul was created, it must die. Some are born happy, enjoy perfect health with beautiful body, mental vigor, and all wants supplied. Others are born miserable; some are without hands or feet; others again are idiots, and only drag on a wretched existence. Why, if they are all created, why does a just and merciful God create one happy and another unhappy, why is He so partial? Nor would it mend matters in the least to hold that those who are miserable in this life will be happy in a one. Why should a man be miserable even here in the reign of a just and merciful God?

In the second place, the idea of a creator God does not explain the anomaly, but simply expresses the cruel Rat of an all-powerful being. There must have been causes, then, before his birth, to make a man miserable or happy and those were his past actions.

Are not all the tendencies of the mind and the body accounted for by inherited aptitude? Here are two parallel lines of existence - one of the mind, the other of matter. If matter and its transformations answer for all that we have, there is no necessity for supposing the existence of a soul. But it cannot be proved that thought has been evolved out of matter; and if a philosophical monism is inevitable, spiritual monism is certainly logical and no less desirable than a materialistic monism; but neither of these is necessary here.

We cannot deny that bodies acquire certain tendencies from heredity, but those tendencies only mean the physical configuration through which a peculiar mind alone can act in a peculiar way. There are other tendencies peculiar to a soul caused by his past actions. And a soul with a certain tendency would, by the laws of affinity, take birth in a body which is the fittest instrument for the display of that tendency. This is in accord with science, for science wants to explain everything by habit, and habit is got through repetitions. So repetitions are necessary to explain the natural habits of a new born soul. And since they were not obtained in this present life, they must have come down from past lives.

There is another suggestion. Taking all these for granted, how is it that I do not remember anything of my past life? This can be easily explained. I am now speaking English. It is not my mother tongue; in fact, no words of my mother tongue are now present in my consciousness; but let me try to bring them up, and they rush in. That shows that consciousness is only the surface of mental ocean, and within its depths are stored up all our experiences. Try and struggle, they would come up. and you would be conscious even of your past life.

This is direct and demonstrative evidence. Verification is the perfect proof of a theory, and here is the challenge thrown to the world by the Rishis. We have discovered the secret by which the very depths of the ocean of memory can be stirred up - try it and you would get a complete reminiscence of your past life.

So then the Hindu believes that he is a spirit. Him the sword cannot pierce - him the fire cannot burn - him the water cannot melt - him the air cannot dry. The Hindu believes that every soul is a circle whose circumference is nowhere but whose center is located in the body, and that death means the change of the center from holy to body. Nor is the soul bound by the conditions of matter.

In its very essence, it is flee, unbounded, holy, pure, and perfect. But somehow or other it finds itself tied down to matter and thinks of itself as matter. Why should the free, perfect, and pure be thus under the thralldom of matter, is the next question. How can the perfect soul be deluded into the belief that it is imperfect? We have been told that the

Hindus shirk the question and say that no such question can be there- Some thinkers want to answer it by positing one or more quasi-perfect beings, and use big scientific names to fill up the gap. But naming is not explaining. The question remains the same. How can the perfect become the quasi-perfect; how can the pure, the absolute change even a microscopic particle of its nature? But the Hindu is sincere. He does not want to take shelter under sophistry. He is brave enough to face the question in a manly fashion; and his answer is: 'I do not know.' I do not know how the perfect being, the soul, came to think of itself as imperfect, as Joined to and conditioned by matter.' But the fact is a fact for all that. It is a fact in everybody's consciousness that one thinks of oneself as the body. The Hindu does not attempt to explain why one thinks one is the body. The answer that it is the will of God is no explanation. This is nothing more than what the Hindu says, 'I do not know.'

Well, then, the human soul is eternal and immortal, perfect and infinite, and death means only a change of center from one body to another. The present is determined by our past actions, and the future by the present. The soul will go on evolving up or reverting back from birth to birth and death to death. But here is another question: Is man a tiny boat in a tempest, raised one moment on the foamy crest of a billow and dashed down into a yawning chasm the next, rolling to and from at the mercy of good and bad actions - a powerless, helpless wreck in an ever-raging, ever-rushing, uncompromising current of cause and effect - a little moth placed under the wheel of causation, which rolls on crushing everything in its way and waits not for the widow's tears or the orphan's cry? The heart sinks at the idea, yet this is the law of nature. Is there no hope? Is there no escape? - was the cry that went up from the bottom of the heart of despair. It reached the throne of mercy, and words of hope and consolation came down and inspired a Vedic sage, and he stood up before the world and in trumpet voice proclaimed the glad tidings: 'Hear, ye children of immortal bliss! even ye that reside in higher spheres! I have found the Ancient One who is beyond all darkness, all delusion: knowing Him alone you shall be saved from death over again. 'Children of immortal bliss' -what a sweet, what a hopeful name! Allow me to call you, brethren, by that sweet name -heirs of immortal bliss - yea, the Hindu refuses to call you sinners. We are the Children of God, the sharers of immortal bliss, holy and perfect beings divinities on earth - sinners! It is a sin to call a ma. so; it is standing libel on human nature. Come up, O lions, and shake off the delusion that you are sheep; you are souls immortal, spirits free, blest and eternal; ye are not matter, ye are not bodies; matter is your servant, not you the servant of matter.

Thus it is that the Vedas proclaim not a dreadful combination of unforgiving laws, not an endless prison of cause and effect, but that at the head of all these laws, in and through every particle of matter and force, stands One, 'by whose command the wind blows, the fire burns, the clouds rain and death stalks upon the earth.'

And what is His nature?

Swami Vivekananda

The World Parliament of Religions, Chicago

CONCLUDING ADDRESS - Chicago, Sept 27, 1893

The World's Parliament of Religions has become an accomplished fact, and the merciful Father has helped those who laboured to bring it into existence, and crowned with success their most unselfish labour.

My thanks to those noble souls whose large hearts and love of truth first dreamed this wonderful dream and then realized it. My thanks to the shower of liberal sentiments that has overflowed this platform. My thanks to this enlightened audience for their uniform kindness to me and for their appreciation of every thought that tends to smooth the friction of religions. A few jarring notes were heard from time to time in this harmony. My special thanks to them, for they have, by their striking contrast, made general harmony the sweeter.

Much has been said of the common ground of religious unity. I am not going just now to venture my own theory. But if anyone here hopes that this unity will come by the triumph of any one of the religions and the destruction of the others, to him I say, "Brother, yours is an impossible hope." Do I wish that the Christian would become Hindu? God forbid. Do I wish that the Hindu or Buddhist would become Christian? God forbid.

The seed is put in the ground, and earth and air and water are placed around it. Does the seed become the earth, or the air, or the water? No. It becomes a plant. It develops after the law of its own growth, assimilates the air, the earth, and the water, converts them into plant substance, and grows into a plant.

Similar is the case with religion. The Christian is not to become a Hindu or a Buddhist, nor a Hindu or a Buddhist to become a Christian. But each must assimilate the spirit of the others and yet preserve his individuality and grow according to his own law of growth.

147

If the Parliament of Religions has shown anything to the world, it is this: It has proved to the world that holiness, purity and charity are not the exclusive possessions of any church in the world, and that every system has produced men and women of the most exalted character. In the face of this evidence, if anybody dreams of the exclusive survival of his own religion and the destruction of the others, I pity him from the bottom of my heart, and point out to him that upon the banner of every religion will soon be written in spite of resistance: "Help and not fight," "Assimilation and not Destruction," "Harmony and Peace and not Dissension."

MAHATMA GANDHI
THE MOMENT OF TRUTH

[September 11,1906]

(at the Empire Theater in Johannesburg, South Africa)

This is an excerpt from Chapter XII:

THE ADVENT OF SATYAGRAHA

Gandhi, M.K., Satyagraha in South Africa (Ahmedabad, 1928 (revised 2nd edition, 1950) pp. 95-102) The meeting was duly held on September 11, 1906. It was attended by delegates from various places in the Transvaal. But I must confess that even I myself had not then understood all the implications of the resolutions I had helped to frame; nor had I gauged all the possible conclusions to which they might lead. The old Empire Theatre was packed from floor to ceiling. I could read in every face the expectation of something strange to be done or to happen. Mr. Abdul Gani, Chairman of the Transvaal British Indian Association, presided. He was one of the oldest Indian residents of the Transvaal, and partner and manager of the Johannesburg branch of the well-known firm of Mamad Kasam Kamrudin. The most important among the resolutions passed by the meeting was the famous Fourth Resolution by which the Indians solemnly determined not to submit to the Ordinance in the event of its becoming law in the teeth of their opposition and to suffer all the penalties attaching to such non-submission. I fully explained this resolution to the meeting and received a patient hearing. The business of the meeting was conducted in Hindi or Gujarati; it was impossible therefore that any one present should not follow the proceedings. For the Tamils and Telugus who did not know Hindi there were Tamil and Telugu speakers who fully explained everything in their respective languages. The resolution was duly proposed, seconded and supported by several speakers one of whom was Sheth Haji Habib. He too was a very old and experienced resident of South Africa and made an impassioned speech. He was deeply moved and went so far as to say that we must pass this resolution with God as witness and must never yield a cowardly submission to such degrading legislation. He then went on solemnly to declare in the name of God that he would never submit to that law, and advised all present to do likewise. Others also delivered powerful and angry speeches in supporting the resolution. When in the course of his speech Sheth Haji Habib came to the solemn declaration, I was at once startled and put on my guard. Only then did I fully realize my own responsibility and the responsibility of the community. The community had passed many a resolution before and amended such resolutions in the light of further reflection or fresh experience. There were cases in which resolutions passed had not been observed by all concerned. Amendments in resolutions and failure to observe resolutions on the part of persons agreeing thereto are ordinary experiences of public life all the world over. But no one ever imports the name of God into such resolutions. In the abstract there should not be any distinction between a resolution and an oath taken in the name of God. When an intelligent man makes a resolution deliberately he never swerves from it by a hair's breadth. With him his resolution carries as much weight as a declaration made with. God as witness does. But the world takes no note of abstract principles and imagines an ordinary resolution and an oath in the name of God to be poles asunder. A man who makes an ordinary resolution is not ashamed of himself when he deviates from it, but a man who violates an oath administered to him is not only ashamed of himself, but is also looked upon by society as sinner. This imaginary distinction has struck such a deep root in the human mind that a person making a statement on oath before a judge is held to have committed an offence in law Ft the statement is proved to be false and receives drastic punishment. Full of these thoughts as I was, possessing as 1 did much experience of solemn pledges, having profited by them, I was taken aback by Sheth Haji Habib's suggestion of an oath. I thought out the possible consequences of it in a moment. My perplexity gave place to enthusiasm. And although I had no intention of taking an oath or inviting others to do so when I went to the meeting, I warmly approved of the Sheth's suggestion. But at the same time it seemed to me that the people should be told of all the consequences and should have explained to them clearly the meaning of a pledge. And if even then they were prepared to pledge themselves, they should be encouraged to do so; otherwise I must understand that they were not still ready to stand the final test. I therefore asked the President for permission to explain to the meeting the implications of Sheth Haji Habib's suggestion. The President readily granted it and I rose to address the meeting. I give below a summary of my remarks just as I can recall them now: "I wish to explain to this meeting that there is a vast difference between this resolution and every other resolution we have passed up to date and that there is a wide divergence also in the manner of making it. It is a very grave resolution we are making, as our existence in South Africa depends upon our fully observing it. The manner of making the resolution suggested by our friend is as much of a novelty as of a solemnity. I did not come to the meeting with a view to getting the resolution passed in that manner, which redounds to the credit of Sheth Haji Habib as well as it lays a burden of responsibility upon him. I tender my congratulations to him. I deeply appreciate his suggestion, but if you adopt it you too will share his responsibility. You must understand what is this responsibility, and as an adviser and servant of the community, it is my duty fully to explain it to you. "We all believe in one and the same God, the differences of nomenclature in Hinduism and Islam notwithstanding. To pledge ourselves or to take an oath in the name of that God or with him as witness is not something to be trifled with. If having taken such an oath we violate our pledge we are guilty before God and man. Personally I hold that a man, who deliberately and intelligently takes a pledge and then breaks it, forfeits his manhood. "And just as a copper coin treated with mercury not only becomes valueless when detected but also makes its owner liable to punishment, in the same way a man who lightly pledges his word and then breaks it becomes a man of straw and fits himself for punishment here as well as hereafter. Sheth Haji Habib is proposing to administer an oath of a very serious character. There is no one in this meeting who can be classed as an infant or as wanting in understanding. You are all well advanced in age and have seen the world; many of you are delegates and have discharged responsibilities in a greater or lesser measure. No one present, therefore, can ever hope to excuse himself by saying that he did not know what he was about when he took the oath. "I know that pledges and vows are, and should be, taken on rare occasions. A man who takes a vow every now and then is sure to stumble. But if I can imagine a crisis in the history of the Indian community of South Africa when it would be in the fitness of things to take pledges that crisis is surely now. There is wisdom in taking serious steps with great caution and hesitation. But caution and hesitation have their limits, and we have now passed them. The Government has taken leave of I all sense of decency. We would only be betraying our unworthiness and cowardice, if we cannot stake our all in the face of the conflagration which envelopes us and sit watching it with folded hands. "There is no doubt, therefore, that the present is a proper occasion for taking pledges. But every one of us must think out for himself if he has the will and the ability to pledge himself. Resolutions of this nature cannot be passed by a majority vote. Only those who take a pledge can be bound by it. This pledge must not be taken with a view to produce an effect on outsiders. No one should trouble to consider what impression it might have upon the Local Government, the Imperial Government, or the Government of India. Everyone must only search his own heart, and if the inner voice assures him that he has the requisite strength to carry him through, then only should he pledge himself and then only will his pledge bear fruit. "A few words now as to the consequences. Hoping I for the best, we may say that if a majority of the Indians pledge themselves to resistance and if all who take the pledge prove true to themselves, the Ordinance may not I be passed and, if passed, may be soon repealed. It may be that we may not be called upon to suffer at all. But if on the one hand a man who takes a pledge must be a robust optimist, on the other hand he must be prepared for the worst. Therefore I want to give you an idea of the worst that might happen to us in the present struggle. "Imagine that all of us present here numbering 3,000 at the most pledge ourselves. Imagine again that the remaining 10,000 Indians take no such pledge. We will only provoke ridicule in the beginning. Again, it is quite possible that in spite of the present warning some or many of those who pledge themselves may weaken at the very first trial. We may have to go to jail, where we may be insulted. We may have to go hungry and suffer extreme heat or cold. Hard labour may be imposed upon us. We may be flogged by rude warders. We may be fined heavily and our property may be attached and held up to auction if there are only a few resisters left. Opulent today we may be reduced to abject poverty tomorrow. We may be deported. Suffering from starvation and similar hardships in jail, some of us may fall ill and even die. In short, therefore, it is not at all impossible that we may have to endure every hardship that we can imagine, and wisdom lies in pledging ourselves on the understanding that we shall have to suffer all that and worse. "If someone asks me when and how the struggle may end, I may say that if the entire community manfully stands the test, the end will be near. If many of us fall back under storm and stress, the struggle will be prolonged. But I can boldly declare, and with certainty, that so long as there is even a handful of men true to their pledge, there can only be one end to the struggle, and that is victory. "A word about my personal responsibility. If I am warning you of the risks attendant upon the pledge, I am at the same time inviting you to pledge yourselves, and I am fully conscious of my responsibility in the matter. It is possible that a majority of those present here may take the pledge in a fit of enthusiasm or indignation but may weaken under the ordeal, and only a handful may be left to face the final test. Even then there is only one course open to someone like me, to die but not to submit to the law. It is quite unlikely but even if everyone else flinched leaving me alone to face the music, I am confident that I would never violate my pledge. "Please do not misunderstand me. I am not saying this out of vanity, but I wish to put you, especially the leaders upon the platform, on your guard. I wish respectfully to suggest it to you that if you have not the will or the ability to stand firm even when you are perfectly isolated, you must not only not take the pledge yourselves but you must declare your opposition before the resolution is put to the meeting and before its members begin to take pledges and you must not make yourselves parties to the resolution. "Although we are going to take the pledge in a body, no one should imagine that default on the part of one or many can absolve the rest from their obligation. Everyone should fully realize his responsibility, then only pledge himself independently of others and understand that he himself must be true to his pledge even unto death, no matter what others do."I spoke to this effect and resumed my seat. The meeting heard me word by word in perfect quiet. Other leaders too spoke. All dwelt upon their own responsibility and the responsibility of the audience. The President rose. He too made the situation clear, and at last all present, standing with upraised hands, took an oath with God as witness not to submit to the Ordinance if it became law. I can never forget the scene, which is present before my mind's eye as I write. The community's enthusiasm knew no bounds. The very next day there was some accident in the theatre in consequence of which it was wholly destroyed by fire. On the third day friends brought me the news of the fire and congratulated the community upon this good omen, which signified to them that the Ordinance would meet the same fate as the theatre. I have never been influenced by such so-called signs and therefore did not attach any weight to the coincidence. I have taken note of it here only as a demonstration of the community's courage and faith. The reader will find in the subsequent chapters many more proofs of these two high qualities of the people. The workers did not let the grass grow under their feet after this great meeting. Meetings were held everywhere and pledges of resistance were taken in every place. The principal topic of discussion in Indian Opinion now was the Black Ordinance. At the other end, steps were taken in order to meet the Local Government. A deputation waited upon Mr. Duncan, the Colonial Secretary, and told him among other things about the pledges. Sheth Haji Habib, who was a member of the deputation, said, 'I cannot possibly restrain myself if any officer comes and proceeds to take my wife's finger prints. I will kill him there and then and die myself.' The Minister stared at the Sheth's face for a while and said, 'Government is reconsidering the advisability of making the Ordinance applicable to women, and I can assure you at once that the clauses relating to women will be deleted. Government have understood your feeling in the matter and desire to respect it. But as for the other provisions, I am sorry to inform you that Government is and will remain adamant. General Botha wants you to agree to this legislation after due deliberation. Government deem it to be essential to the existence of the Europeans. They will certainly consider any suggestions about details which you may make consistently with the objects of the Ordinance, and my advice to the deputation is that your interest lies in agreeing to the legislation and proposing changes only as regards the details.' I am leaving out here the particulars of the discussion with the Minister, as all those arguments have already been dealt with. The arguments were just the same, there was only a difference in phraseology as they were set forth before the Minister. The deputation withdrew, after informing him that his advice notwithstanding, acquiescence in the proposed legislation was out of the question, and after thanking Government for its intention of exempting women from its provisions. It is difficult to say whether the exemption of women was the first fruit of the community's agitation, or whether the Government as an afterthought made a concession to practical considerations which

Mr. Curtis had ruled out of his scientific methods. Government claimed that it had decided to exempt women independently of the Indian agitation. Be that as it might, the community established to their own satisfaction a cause and effect relation between the agitation and the exemption and their fighting spirit rose accordingly. None of us knew what name to give to our movement. I then used the term 'passive resistance' in describing it. I did not quite understand the implications of 'passive resistance' as I called it. I only knew that some new principle had come into being. As the struggle advanced, the phrase 'passive resistance' gave rise to confusion and it appeared shameful to permit this great struggle to be known only by an English name. Again, that foreign phrase could hardly pass as current coin among the community. A small prize was therefore announced in Indian Opinion to be awarded to the reader who invented the best designation for our struggle. We thus received a number of suggestions. The meaning of the struggle had been then fully discussed in Indian Opinion and the competitors for the prize had fairly sufficient material to serve as a basis for their exploration. Shri Maganlal Gandhi was one of the competitors and he suggested the word 'Sadagraha,' meaning 'firmness in a good cause.' I liked the word, but it did not fully represent the whole idea I wished it to connote. I therefore corrected it to 'Satyagraha.' Truth (Satya) implies love, and firmness (agraha) engenders and therefore serves as a synonym for force. I thus began to call the Indian movement 'Satyagraha,' that is to say, the Force which is born of Truth and Love or non-violence, and gave up the use of the phrase 'passive resistance,' in connection with it, so much so that even in English writing we often avoided it and used instead the word 'Satyagraha' itself or some other equivalent English phrase. This then was the genesis of the movement which came to be known as Satyagraha, and of the word used as a designation for it. Before we proceed any further with our history we shall do well to grasp the differences between passive resistance and Satyagraha, which is the subject of our next chapter.

Reference:

1. http://salsa.net/peace/satyagraha/chapterxii.html

2. http://salsa.net/peace/satyagraha/index.html

APPENDIX V

Quotes From Mahatma Gandhi

Mahatma Mohandas Karamchand Gandhi is the greatest of men who have walked the face of this earth !!

Question: Gandhiji, why do you always travel third class?
Answer: because there is no fourth class.

The way to God is to free oneself from possessions and passions.

All through history the way of truth and love has always won in the end: There have been tyrants and murderers who for a time seem invincible but in the end they always fall.

Ahimsa is our Dharma; for Humans to be violent is to reverse the course of evolution and go against their nature which is to love, to endure, to forgive.

What difference does it make to the dead, the orphans and the homeless, whether the mad destruction is wrought under the name of totalitarianism or the holy name of liberty or democracy?

A religion that does not take into account of practical affairs and does not help to solve them is no religion.

Strength does not come from physical capacity but from an indomitable will. Freedom is not worth having if it does not connote freedom to err. It passes my comprehension how human beings, be they ever so experienced and able, can delight in depriving other human beings of that precious right. If you are a minority of one the truth is the truth.

Talisman

I will give you a talisman. Whenever you are in doubt, or when the self becomes too much with you, apply the following test. Recall the face of the poorest and the weakest man [woman] whom you may have seen, and ask yourself, if the step you contemplate is going to be of any use to him [her]. Will he [she] gain anything by it? Will it restore him [her] to a control over his [her] own life and destiny? In other words, will it lead to swaraj [freedom] for the hungry and spiritually starving millions?

Then you will find your doubts and yourself melt away.

- One of the last notes left behind by Gandhi in 1948, expressing his deepest social thought.

A coward is incapable of exhibiting love; it is the prerogative of the brave.

A man is but the product of his thoughts what he thinks, he becomes.

A nation's culture resides in the hearts and in the soul of its people.

A small body of determined spirits fired by an unquenchable faith in their mission can alter the course of history.

A vow is a purely religious act which cannot be taken in a fit of passion. It can be taken only with a mind purified and composed and with God as witness.

A weak man is just by accident. A strong but non-violent man is unjust by accident.

Action expresses priorities.

All compromise is based on give and take, but there can be no give and take on fundamentals. Any compromise on mere fundamentals is a surrender. For it is all give and no take.

All the religions of the world, while they may differ in other respects, unitedly proclaim that nothing lives in this world but Truth.

Always aim at complete harmony of thought and word and deed. Always aim at purifying your thoughts and everything will be well.

An error does not become truth by reason of multiplied propagation, nor does truth become error because nobody sees it.

An ounce of practice is worth more than tons of preaching.

An unjust law is itself a species of violence. Arrest for its breach is more so.

Anger and intolerance are the enemies of correct understanding.

Capital as such is not evil; it is its wrong use that is evil. Capital in some form or other will always be needed.

Confession of errors is like a broom which sweeps away the dirt and leaves the surface brighter and clearer. I feel stronger for confession.

Each one has to find his peace from within. And peace to be real must be unaffected by outside circumstances.

Even if you are a minority of one, the truth is the truth.

Every formula of every religion has in this age of reason, to submit to the acid test of reason and universal assent.

Faith... must be enforced by reason... when faith becomes blind it dies.

Fear has its use but cowardice has none.

First they ignore you, then they laugh at you, then they fight you, then you win.

Freedom is not worth having if it does not connote freedom to err.

Gentleness, self-sacrifice and generosity are the exclusive possession of no one race or religion.

Glory lies in the attempt to reach one's goal and not in reaching it.

God is, even though the whole world deny him. Truth stands, even if there be no public support. It is self-sustained.

Honest disagreement is often a good sign of progress.

I am prepared to die, but there is no cause for which I am prepared to kill.

I believe in the fundamental truth of all great religions of the world.

I claim that human mind or human society is not divided into watertight compartments called social, political and religious. All act and react upon one another.

I claim to be a simple individual liable to err like any other fellow mortal. I own, however, that I have humility enough to confess my errors and to retrace my steps.

I do not want to foresee the future. I am concerned with taking care of the present. God has given me no control over the moment following.

I have nothing new to teach the world. Truth and Non-violence are as old as the hills. All I have done is to try experiments in both on as vast a scale as I could.

I have worshipped woman as the living embodiment of the spirit of service and sacrifice.

I know, to banish anger altogether from one's breast is a difficult task. It cannot be achieved through pure personal effort. It can be done only by God's grace.

I like your Christ, I do not like your Christians. Your Christians are so unlike your Christ.

I object to violence because when it appears to do good, the good is only temporary; the evil it does is permanent.

I reject any religious doctrine that does not appeal to reason and is in conflict with morality.

I will far rather see the race of man extinct than that we should become less than beasts by making the noblest of God's creation, woman, and the object of our lust.

I would heartily welcome the union of East and West provided it is not based on brute force.

If co-operation is a duty, I hold that non-co-operation also under certain conditions is equally a duty.

If I had no sense of humor, I would long ago have committed suicide.

If patience is worth anything, it must endure to the end of time. And a living faith will last in the midst of the blackest storm.

In matters of conscience, the law of the majority has no place.

Infinite striving to be the best is man's duty; it is its own reward. Everything else is in God's hands.

Interdependence is and ought to be as much the ideal of man as self-sufficiency.

Intolerance is itself a form of violence and an obstacle to the growth of a true democratic spirit.

It is any day better to stand erect with a broken and bandaged head then to crawl on one's belly, in order to be able to save one's head.

It is better to be violent, if there is violence in our hearts, than to put on the cloak of nonviolence to cover impotence.

It is health that is real wealth and not pieces of gold and silver.

It is my own firm belief that the strength of the soul grows in proportion as you subdue the flesh.

It is the quality of our work which will please God and not the quantity.

Just as a man would not cherish living in a body other than his own, so do nations not like to live under other nations, however noble and great the latter may be.

Let everyone try and find that as a result of daily prayer he adds something new to his life, something with which nothing can be compared.

Let us all be brave enough to die the death of a martyr, but let no one lust for martyrdom.

Live as if you were to die tomorrow. Learn as if you were to live forever.

Man falls from the pursuit of the ideal of plan living and high thinking the moment he wants to multiply his daily wants. Man's happiness really lies in contentment.

Man lives freely only by his readiness to die, if need be, at the hands of his brother, never by killing him.

Man should forget his anger before he lies down to sleep.

Man's nature is not essentially evil. Brute nature has been known to yield to the influence of love. You must never despair of human nature.

Moral authority is never retained by any attempt to hold on to it. It comes without seeking and is retained without effort.

My life is my message.

My religion is based on truth and non-violence. Truth is my God. Non-violence is the means of realizing Him.

No culture can live if it attempts to be exclusive.

Nobody can hurt me without my permission.

Non-cooperation with evil is as much a duty as is cooperation with good.

Non-violence and truth are inseparable and presuppose one another.

Non-violence is not a garment to be put on and off at will. Its seat is in the heart, and it must be an inseparable part of our being.

Non-violence is the greatest force at the disposal of mankind. It is mightier than the mightiest weapon of destruction devised by the ingenuity of man.

Non-violence requires a double faith, faith in God and also faith in man.

Peace is its own reward.

Poverty is the worst form of violence.

Power is of two kinds. One is obtained by the fear of punishment and the other by acts of love. Power based on love is a thousand times more effective and permanent then the one derived from fear of punishment.

Prayer is not asking. It is a longing of the soul. It is daily admission of one's weakness. It is better in prayer to have a heart without words than words without a heart.

Prayer is the key of the morning and the bolt of the evening.

Purity of personal life is the one indispensable condition for building up a sound education.

Religion is a matter of the heart. No physical inconvenience can warrant abandonment of one's own religion.

Religion is more than life. Remember that his own religion is the truest to every man even if it stands low in the scales of philosophical comparison.

Satisfaction lies in the effort, not in the attainment, full effort is full victory.

Service which is rendered without joy helps neither the servant nor the served. But all other pleasures and possessions pale into nothingness before service which is rendered in a spirit of joy.

Spiritual relationship is far more precious than physical. Physical relationship divorced from spiritual is body without soul.

Strength does not come from physical capacity. It comes from an indomitable will.

That service is the noblest which is rendered for its own sake.

The difference between what we do and what we are capable of doing would suffice to solve most of the world's problem.

The essence of all religions is one. Only their approaches are different.

The good man is the friend of all living things.

The human voice can never reach the distance that is covered by the still small voice of conscience.

The main purpose of life is to live rightly, think rightly, and act rightly.

The soul must languish when we give all our thought to the body.

The moment there is suspicion about a person's motives, everything he does becomes tainted.

The only tyrant I accept in this world is the still voice within.

The pursuit of truth does not permit violence on one's opponent.

The real ornament of woman is her character, her purity.

There are people in the world so hungry, that God cannot appear to them except in the form of bread.

There is a higher court than courts of justice and that is the court of conscience. It supercedes all other courts.

There is an orderliness in the universe, there is an unalterable law governing everything and every being that exists or lives. It is no blind law; for no blind law can govern the conduct of living beings.

Those who know how to think need no teachers.

Those who say religion has nothing to do with politics do not know what religion is.

To believe in something, and not to live it, is dishonest.

To deprive a man of his natural liberty and to deny to him the ordinary amenities of life is worse than starving the body; it is starvation of the soul, the dweller in the body.

Truth never damages a cause that is just.

Truth stands, even if there be no public support. It is self-sustained.

Unwearied ceaseless effort is the price that must be paid for turning faith into a rich infallible experience.

Violent means will give violent freedom. That would be a menace to the world ....

We do not need to proselytise either by our speech or by our writing. We can only do so really with our lives. Let our lives be open books for all to study.

We may never be strong enough to be entirely nonviolent in thought, word and deed. But we must keep nonviolence as our goal and make strong progress towards it.

We should meet abuse by forbearance. Human nature is so constituted that if we take absolutely no notice of anger or abuse, the person indulging in it will soon weary of it and stop.

We win justice quickest by rendering justice to the other party.

What difference does it make to the dead, the orphans, and the homeless, whether the mad destruction is wrought under the name of totalitarianism or the holy name of liberty or democracy?

What do I think of Western civilization? I think it would be a very good idea.

What is true of the individual will be tomorrow true of the whole nation if individuals will but refuse to lose heart and hope.

Whatever you do may seem insignificant to you, but it is most important that you do it.

When restraint and courtesy are added to strength, the latter becomes irresistible.

Where there is love there is life.

You can chain me, you can torture me, you can even destroy this body, but you will never imprison my mind.

http://www.brainyquote.com/quotes/authors/m/
mohandas_gandhi_10.html
http://mkgandhi.org/epigrams/y.htm

APPENDIX VI

Matthew 5

The Sermon on the Mount

¹ Now when Jesus saw the crowds, he went up on a mountainside and sat down. His disciples came to him, ² and he began to teach them.

The Beatitudes

He said:

³ "Blessed are the poor in spirit, for theirs is the kingdom of heaven.

⁴ Blessed are those who mourn, for they will be comforted.

⁵ Blessed are the meek, for they will inherit the earth.

⁶ Blessed are those who hunger and thirst for righteousness, for they will be filled.

⁷ Blessed are the merciful, for they will be shown mercy.

⁸ Blessed are the pure in heart, for they will see God.

⁹ Blessed are the peacemakers, for they will be called children of God.

¹⁰ Blessed are those who are persecuted because of righteousness, for theirs is the kingdom of heaven.

¹¹ Blessed are you when people insult you, persecute you and falsely say all kinds of evil against you because of me.

¹² Rejoice and be glad, because great is your reward in heaven, for in the same way they persecuted the prophets who were before you."

Salt and Light

¹³ "You are the salt of the earth. But if the salt loses its saltiness, how can it be made salty again? It is no longer good for anything, except to be thrown out and trampled underfoot.

¹⁴ You are the light of the world. A town built on a hill cannot be hidden.

¹⁵ Neither do people light a lamp and put it under a bowl. Instead they put it on its stand, and it gives light to everyone in the house.

¹⁶ In the same way, let your light shine before others, that they may see your good deeds and glorify your Father in heaven."

The Fulfillment of the Law

¹⁷ "Do not think that I have come to abolish the Law or the Prophets; I have not come to abolish them but to fulfill them.

¹⁸ For truly I tell you, until heaven and earth disappear, not the smallest letter, not the least stroke of a pen, will by any means disappear from the Law until everything is accomplished.

¹⁹ Therefore anyone who sets aside one of the least of these commands and teaches others accordingly will be called least in the kingdom of heaven, but whoever practices and teaches these commands will be called great in the kingdom of heaven.

²⁰ For I tell you that unless your righteousness surpasses that of the Pharisees and the teachers of the law, you will certainly not enter the kingdom of heaven."

Murder

²¹ "You have heard that it was said to the people long ago, 'You shall not murder, and anyone who murders will be subject to judgment.'

²² But I tell you that anyone who is angry with a brother or sister will be subject to judgment. Again, anyone who says to a brother or sister, 'Raca,' is answerable to the court. And anyone who says, 'You fool!' will be in danger of the fire of hell.

²³ Therefore, if you are offering your gift at the altar and there remember that your brother or sister has something against you,

²⁴ Leave your gift there in front of the altar. First go and be reconciled to them; then come and offer your gift.

²⁵ Settle matters quickly with your adversary who is taking you to court. Do it while you are still together on the way, or your adversary may hand you over to the judge, and the judge may hand you over to the officer, and you may be thrown into prison.

²⁶ Truly I tell you, you will not get out until you have paid the last penny.

Adultery

²⁷ "You have heard that it was said, 'You shall not commit adultery.'

²⁸ But I tell you that anyone who looks at a woman lustfully has already committed adultery with her in his heart.

²⁹ If your right eye causes you to stumble, gouge it out and throw it away. It is better for you to lose one part of your body than for your whole body to be thrown into hell.

³⁰ And if your right hand causes you to stumble, cut it off and throw it away. It is better for you to lose one part of your body than for your whole body to go into hell."

Divorce

³¹ "It has been said, 'Anyone who divorces his wife must give her a certificate of divorce.'

³² But I tell you that anyone who divorces his wife, except for sexual immorality, makes her the victim of adultery, and anyone who marries a divorced woman commits adultery."

Oaths

³³ "Again, you have heard that it was said to the people long ago, 'Do not break your oath, but fulfill to the Lord the vows you have made.'

³⁴ But I tell you, do not swear an oath at all: either by heaven, for it is God's throne;

³⁵ Or by the earth, for it is his footstool; or by Jerusalem, for it is the city of the Great King.

³⁶ And do not swear by your head, for you cannot make even one hair white or black.

³⁷ All you need to say is simply 'Yes' or 'No'; anything beyond this comes from the evil one."

Eye for Eye

[38] "You have heard that it was said, 'Eye for eye, and tooth for tooth.'

[39] But I tell you, do not resist an evil person. If anyone slaps you on the right cheek, turn to them the other cheek also.

[40] And if anyone wants to sue you and take your shirt, hand over your coat as well.

[41] If anyone forces you to go one mile, go with them two miles.

[42] Give to the one who asks you, and do not turn away from the one who wants to borrow from you."

Love for Enemies

[43] "You have heard that it was said, 'Love your neighbor and hate your enemy.'

[44] But I tell you, love your enemies and pray for those who persecute you,

[45] That you may be children of your Father in heaven. He causes his sun to rise on the evil and the good, and sends rain on the righteous and the unrighteous.

[46] If you love those who love you, what reward will you get? Are not even the tax collectors doing that?

[47] And if you greet only your own people, what are you doing more than others? Do not even pagans do that?

[48] Be perfect, therefore, as your heavenly Father is perfect.

APPENDIX VII

Universality of the Golden Rule

"We have committed the Golden Rule to memory; let us now commit it to life."

Edwin Markham

Religious Beliefs Governing Behavior Toward Other People

Faith groups differ greatly in their concepts of deity, other beliefs and practices. But there is near unanimity of opinion among the world's various historical religions on how one person should treat another. Almost all religions have passages in their holy texts, or writings of their leaders, which promote the *Ethic of Reciprocity* or the *Golden Rule*.

Baha'i Faith "Lay not on any soul a load that you would not wish to be laid upon you, and desire not for anyone the things you would not desire for yourself."

"Ascribe not to any soul that which thou wouldst not have ascribed to thee, and say not that which thou does not." "Blessed is he who preferreth his brother before himself." (Baha'u'llah, Gleanings, LXVI:8)

Brahmanism "This is the sum of duty: do naught unto others which would cause you pain if done to you." (Mahabharata 5:1517)

Buddhism "Hurt not others in ways that your yourself would find hurtful." (Udana-Varga 5.18)

"A state that is not pleasing or delightful to me, how could I inflict that upon another?" (Samyutta Nikaya v. 353)

Christianity "Do unto others as you would have them do unto you." (Matthew 7:12)

"...and do not do what you hate..." (Gospel of Thomas 6)

Confucianism "Surely it is the maxim of loving-kindness: Do not do to others what you would not have them do to you." (Analects 15:23)

"Tse-kung asked, 'Is there one word that can serve as a principle of conduct for life?' Confucius replied, 'It is the word 'shu' — reciprocity. Do not impose on others what you yourself do not desire.'" (Doctrine of the Mean 13.3)

Hinduism "Do not do to others what would cause pain if done to you. " (Mahabharata 5.1517)

"One should not behave towards others in a way which is disagreeable to oneself." (Mencius Vii.A.4)

Islam "Not one of you is a believer until you wish for others what you wish for yourself." (Fourth Hadith of an-Nawawi 13)

"No one of you is a believer until he desires for his brother that which he desires for himself." (Sunnah)

Jainism "One should treat all creatures in the world as one would like to be treated." (Mahavira, Sutrakritamga)

"Therefore, neither does he [, a sage,] cause violence to others nor does he make others do so." (Acarangasutra 5.101-2)

"In happiness and suffering, in joy and grief, we should regard all creatures as we regard our own self." (Lord Mahavira, 24th Tirthankara)

Judaism "What is hateful to you, do not do to your neighbor." (Talmud, Shabbat 31a; Tobit 4:15)

"...thou shalt love thy neighbor as thyself." (Leviticus 19:18)

Native American Spirituality "Humankind has not woven the web of life. We are but one thread within it. Whatever we do to the web, we do to ourselves." (Chief Seattle) "Respect for all life is the foundation." (The Great Law of Peace)

Paganism (Roman) "The law imprinted on the hearts of all men is to love the members of society as themselves."

Scientology "Try not to do things to others that you would not like them to do to you."

"Try to treat others as you would want them to treat you." (The Way to Happiness by L. Ron Hubbard)

Shintoism "Hurt not others with that which pains yourself." (Udana-Varga 5.18)

"The heart of the person before you is a mirror. See there your own form."

Sikhism "Don't create enmity with anyone as God is within everyone." (Guru Granth Sahib, pg. 1299; Guru Arjan Devji 259)

"Compassion-mercy and religion are the support of the entire world." (Guru Japji Sahib)

Sufism "The basis of Sufism is consideration of the hearts and feelings of others. If you haven't the will to gladden someone's heart, then at least beware lest you hurt someone's heart, for on our path, no sin exists but this." (Dr. Javad Nurbakhsh, Master of the Nimatullahi Sufi Order)

Taoism "Regard your neighbor's gain as your own gain and regard your neighbor's loss as your own loss." (Tai Shang kan Ying P'ien, 213 - 218)

"I am good to the man who is good to me, likewise, I am also good to the bad man." (Tao Te Ching)

Unitarianism "We affirm and promote respect for the interdependent web of all existence of which we are a part." (Unitarian principle)

Wicca "A'in it harm no one, do what thou wilt" (i.e., do whatever you want to, as long as it harms nobody, including yourself). (The Wiccan Rede)

Yoruba (Nigeria) "One going to take a pointed stick to pinch a baby bird should first try it on himself to feel how it hurts."

Zoroastrianism "Do not do unto others whatever is injurious to yourself." (Shayast-na-Shayast, 13.29)

"That nature alone is good which refrains from doing unto another whatsoever is not good for itself.

APPENDIX VIII

UNITED NATIONS

The Universal Declaration of Human Rights

Universal Values

The core principles of human rights first set out in the UDHR, such as universality, interdependence and indivisibility, equality and non-discrimination, and that human rights simultaneously entail both rights and obligations from duty bearers and rights owners, have been reiterated in numerous international human rights conventions, declarations, and resolutions. Today, all United Nations member States have ratified at least one of the nine core international human rights treaties, and 80 percent have ratified four or more, giving concrete expression to the universality of the UDHR and international human rights.

How Does International Law Protect Human Rights?

International human rights law lays down obligations which States are bound to respect. By becoming parties to international treaties, States assume obligations and duties under international law to respect, to protect and to fulfill human rights. The obligation to respect means that States must refrain from interfering with or curtailing the enjoyment of human rights. The obligation to protect requires States to protect individuals and groups against human rights abuses. The obligation to fulfill means that States must take positive action to facilitate the enjoyment of basic human rights.

Through ratification of international human rights treaties, Governments undertake to put into place domestic measures and legislation compatible with their treaty obligations and duties. The domestic legal system, therefore, provides the principal legal protection of human rights guaranteed under international law. Where domestic legal proceedings fail to address human rights abuses, mechanisms and procedures for individual and group complaints are available at the regional and international levels to help ensure that international human rights standards are indeed respected, implemented, and enforced at the local level.

PREAMBLE

Whereas recognition of the inherent dignity and of the equal and inalienable rights of all members of the human family is the foundation of freedom, justice and peace in the world,

Whereas disregard and contempt for human rights have resulted in barbarous acts which have outraged the conscience of mankind, and the advent of a world in which human beings shall enjoy freedom of speech and belief and freedom from fear and want has been proclaimed as the highest aspiration of the common people,

Whereas it is essential, if man is not to be compelled to have recourse, as a last resort, to rebellion against tyranny and oppression, that human rights should be protected by the rule of law,

Whereas it is essential to promote the development of friendly relations between nations,

Whereas the peoples of the United Nations have in the Charter reaffirmed their faith in fundamental human rights, in the dignity and worth of the human person and in the equal rights of men and women and have determined to promote social progress and better standards of life in larger freedom,

Whereas Member States have pledged themselves to achieve, in co-operation with the United Nations, the promotion of universal respect for and observance of human rights and fundamental freedoms,

Whereas a common understanding of these rights and freedoms is of the greatest importance for the full realization of this pledge,

Now, Therefore THE GENERAL ASSEMBLY proclaims THIS UNIVERSAL DECLARATION OF HUMAN RIGHTS as a common standard of achievement for all peoples and all nations, to the end that every individual and every organ of society, keeping this Declaration constantly in mind, shall strive by teaching and education to promote respect for these rights and freedoms and by progressive measures, national and international, to secure their universal and effective recognition and observance, both among the peoples of Member States themselves and among the peoples of territories under their jurisdiction:

Article 1.

- All human beings are born free and equal in dignity and rights. They are endowed with reason and conscience and should act towards one another in a spirit of brotherhood.

Article 2.

- Everyone is entitled to all the rights and freedoms set forth in this Declaration, without distinction of any kind, such as race, colour, sex, language, religion, political or other opinion, national or social origin, property, birth or other status. Furthermore, no distinction shall be made on the basis of the political, jurisdictional or international status of the country or territory to which a person belongs, whether it be independent, trust, non-self-governing or under any other limitation of sovereignty.

Article 3.

- Everyone has the right to life, liberty and security of person.

Article 4.

- No one shall be held in slavery or servitude; slavery and the slave trade shall be prohibited in all their forms.

Article 5.

- No one shall be subjected to torture or to cruel, inhuman or degrading treatment or punishment.

Article 6.

- Everyone has the right to recognition everywhere as a person before the law.

Article 7.

- All are equal before the law and are entitled without any discrimination to equal protection of the law. All are entitled to equal protection against any discrimination in violation of this Declaration and against any incitement to such discrimination.

Article 8.

- Everyone has the right to an effective remedy by the competent national tribunals for acts violating the fundamental rights granted him by the constitution or by law.

Article 9.

- No one shall be subjected to arbitrary arrest, detention or exile.

Article 10.

- Everyone is entitled in full equality to a fair and public hearing by an independent and impartial tribunal, in the determination of his rights and obligations and of any criminal charge against him.

Article 11.

- (1) Everyone charged with a penal offence has the right to be presumed innocent until proved guilty according to law in a public trial at which he has had all the guarantees necessary for his defence.

- (2) No one shall be held guilty of any penal offence on account of any act or omission which did not constitute a penal offence, under national or international law, at the time when it was committed. Nor shall a heavier penalty be imposed than the one that was applicable at the time the penal offence was committed.

Article 12.

- No one shall be subjected to arbitrary interference with his privacy, family, home or correspondence, nor to attacks upon his honour and reputation. Everyone has the right to the protection of the law against such interference or attacks.

Article 13.

- (1) Everyone has the right to freedom of movement and residence within the borders of each state.

- (2) Everyone has the right to leave any country, including his own, and to return to his country.

Article 14.

- (1) Everyone has the right to seek and to enjoy in other countries asylum from persecution.

- (2) This right may not be invoked in the case of prosecutions genuinely arising from non-political crimes or from acts contrary to the purposes and principles of the United Nations.

Article 15.

- (1) Everyone has the right to a nationality.
- (2) No one shall be arbitrarily deprived of his nationality nor denied the right to change his nationality.

Article 16.

- (1) Men and women of full age, without any limitation due to race, nationality or religion, have the right to marry and to found a family. They are entitled to equal rights as to marriage, during marriage and at its dissolution.
- (2) Marriage shall be entered into only with the free and full consent of the intending spouses.
- (3) The family is the natural and fundamental group unit of society and is entitled to protection by society and the State.

Article 17.

- (1) Everyone has the right to own property alone as well as in association with others.
- (2) No one shall be arbitrarily deprived of his property.

Article 18.

- Everyone has the right to freedom of thought, conscience and religion; this right includes freedom to change his religion or belief, and freedom, either alone or in community with others and in public or private, to manifest his religion or belief in teaching, practice, worship and observance.

Article 19.

- Everyone has the right to freedom of opinion and expression; this right includes freedom to hold opinions without interference and to seek, receive and impart information and ideas through any media and regardless of frontiers.

Article 20.

- (1) Everyone has the right to freedom of peaceful assembly and association.
- (2) No one may be compelled to belong to an association.

Article 21.

- (1) Everyone has the right to take part in the government of his country, directly or through freely chosen representatives.

- (2) Everyone has the right of equal access to public service in his country.

- (3) The will of the people shall be the basis of the authority of government; this will shall be expressed in periodic and genuine elections which shall be by universal and equal suffrage and shall be held by secret vote or by equivalent free voting procedures.

Article 22.

- Everyone, as a member of society, has the right to social security and is entitled to realization, through national effort and international co-operation and in accordance with the organization and resources of each State, of the economic, social and cultural rights indispensable for his dignity and the free development of his personality.

Article 23.

- (1) Everyone has the right to work, to free choice of employment, to just and favourable conditions of work and to protection against unemployment.

- (2) Everyone, without any discrimination, has the right to equal pay for equal work.

- (3) Everyone who works has the right to just and favourable remuneration ensuring for himself and his family an existence worthy of human dignity, and supplemented, if necessary, by other means of social protection.

- (4) Everyone has the right to form and to join trade unions for the protection of his interests.

Article 24.

- Everyone has the right to rest and leisure, including reasonable limitation of working hours and periodic holidays with pay.

Article 25.

- (1) Everyone has the right to a standard of living adequate for the health and well-being of himself and of his family, including food, clothing, housing and medical care and necessary social services, and the right to security in the event of unemployment, sickness, disability, widowhood, old age or other lack of livelihood in circumstances beyond his control.

- (2) Motherhood and childhood are entitled to special care and assistance. All children, whether born in or out of wedlock, shall enjoy the same social protection.

Article 26.

- (1) Everyone has the right to education. Education shall be free, at least in the elementary and fundamental stages. Elementary education shall be compulsory. Technical and professional education shall be made generally available and higher education shall be equally accessible to all on the basis of merit.

- (2) Education shall be directed to the full development of the human personality and to the strengthening of respect for human rights and fundamental freedoms. It shall promote understanding, tolerance and friendship among all nations, racial or religious groups, and shall further the activities of the United Nations for the maintenance of peace.

- (3) Parents have a prior right to choose the kind of education that shall be given to their children.

Article 27.

- (1) Everyone has the right freely to participate in the cultural life of the community, to enjoy the arts and to share in scientific advancement and its benefits.

- (2) Everyone has the right to the protection of the moral and material interests resulting from any scientific, literary or artistic production of which he is the author.

Article 28.

- Everyone is entitled to a social and international order in which the rights and freedoms set forth in this Declaration can be fully realized.

Article 29.

- (1) Everyone has duties to the community in which alone the free and full development of his personality is possible.

- (2) In the exercise of his rights and freedoms, everyone shall be subject only to such limitations as are determined by law solely for the purpose of securing due recognition and respect for the rights and freedoms of others and of meeting the just requirements of morality, public order and the general welfare in a democratic society.

- (3) These rights and freedoms may in no case be exercised contrary to the purposes and principles of the United Nations.

Article 30.

- Nothing in this Declaration may be interpreted as implying for any State, group or person any right to engage in any activity or to perform any act aimed at the destruction of any of the rights and freedoms set forth herein.

Reference: Online : http://www.un.org/en/documents/udhr/

Index

A

B

About the Author

Ramnarine Sahadeo, (Ramji) completed his B.A. in 1972 from California State University, Pomona. That same year he moved to Canada where he obtained his LLB at University of Windsor, Ontario. He has been practicing Family, Criminal, and Immigration Law in the Greater Toronto area since 1980.

The events of September 11, 2001, have caused him to reflect on life and the changes that continue to influence people and nations all over the globe. His experience in the courts and administrative tribunals, particularly those dealing with immigrants, and his travels outside Canada have all provided motivation for this work. He can write volumes on just his experience as a brown man with a beard, but that will not result in any significant change to those who judge on appearance.

What he thinks will make a difference is to remind the world of other peaceful events that took place on that date in history so that mankind learns to not only understand and get along with each other, but also get ahead, hopefully, with more spiritual guidance. This is not to say that man must not live and must not oppose injustice, but he can do so by peaceful means. In fact, he hopes that this book will remind readers of other 9/11s, namely, 1893 and 1906, which also had a great impact on world history but which were nonviolent and appealed for universal brotherhood.

He is concerned that citizens of most Western nations now have less freedom and rights because of fear of more violent actions and that those rights will not be returned. It is incumbent on us all to prevent the birth or nourishment of thoughts, words, and deeds associated with violence while confronting injustice.

This book is his humble contribution.

He was born in Guyana (formerly British Guyana) on the island of Leguan situated at the mouth of the giant Essequibo River that flows into the Atlantic Ocean. His father, called Jahaji, died when Ramji was one year-old, leaving his widowed mother in a rural agricultural community to fend for herself and six infant children, the eldest being thirteen years of age. Ramji cherishes his early years and feels indebted to the Hindu community, whose values and lifestyles created a kind of "Ram Raj." His ancestors came from India to Guyana as indentured servants, starting with the arrival of the first ships, *Whitby* and *Hesperus*, on May 5, 1838.

Prominent concepts in the Gita like duty, karma, seva, and belief in reincarnation all helped his late mother, who could not read or write, to fulfill her duty to her family and the community, even though she was a widow for 50 years in what was essentially a "man's world."

It is important to Ramji that he was born nine months before Mahatma Gandhi was assassinated on January 30, 1948, as many are already questioning whether that great soul actually graced this earth. He takes pride in the fact that like the Mahatma, his interest in the Bhagavad-Gita started growing as he became more and more disillusioned with the world he experienced as a young idealistic lawyer. He often mused how different history may have been if the British had just appointed Gandhi a judge.

Like Mahatma Gandhi, though born in a Hindu family, Ramji did not read the Bhagavad-Gita in his early years. In fact, no such books were readily available in the villages in which he grew up. Only special people had access to one. He hopes to change that.

He is positive that the entire justice systems in most democratic countries would have need for less resources if residents can just heed chapter 16:21 of the Gita and avoid lust, anger, and greed, for these vices clog the courts with expensive, unpredictable, and unnecessary litigation.

The health and social systems experience lower demands from those who exercise, perform yoga, and meditate or follow a vegetarian diet, practices followed by Gandhi and recommended by the Gita.

He is keenly aware that even though Gandhi never visited South America or the Caribbean, his efforts with others to end indentureship in 1917 changed the lives of many who did not return to India, but who continued to live in another world still guided by his life and the eternal teachings of the Gita.

It is the author's hope that this book will appeal to all irrespective of age, nationality, or religious affiliation.

Positive change in this world must begin with each person. Each of us can begin to meditate or even be silent for a few hours a day; live a simple and humble lifestyle; practice nonviolence in thoughts, words, and deeds; be a vegetarian; refuse to participate in coercive conversion as it is still one of the major sources of conflict and we are all children of the same source of divine energy. We can do it all with a childlike sense of humor of Gandhi as our world is badly in need of a few more *great souls.*

As a founding member of Sanatan Dharma Educational Foundation of Canada, Ramji hopes that universal Vedic principles will help all realize their divine potential as caring and compassionate souls who can contribute in a significant way to the well-being of themselves and to any countries they choose to call home. This knowledge should be shared as a gift for all mankind since it must survive the materialism that enslaves the divinity inherent in us all.

Those wishing to promote this knowledge can visit :
ramjihindu@rogers.com